Spies, Pop Flies, and French Fries

Spies, Pop Flies, and French Fries

STORIES I TOLD MY FAVORITE VISITORS TO THE CIA EXHIBIT CENTER

By
Linda McCarthy

History is a Hoot, Inc.
Markham, Virginia

Printed and bound in the United States of America

The author and publisher have made every effort to
ensure the accuracy and completeness of information
contained in this book. Any slights of people, places,
or organizations are unintentional.

Publisher's Cataloging-in-Publication
(Provided by Quality Books, Inc.)

McCarthy, Linda, 1950-
Spies, pop flies, and French fries : stories
I told my favorite visitors to the CIA exhibit
center / by Linda McCarthy. — 1st ed.
p. cm.
Includes index.
LCCN: 98-89629
ISBN: 0-9669538-0-0

1. United States. Central Intelligence
Agency—History. I. Title.

JK468.I6M32 1999 327.1273'09
QBI99-177

HOW TO ORDER:

Additional copies of *Spies, Pop Flies, and French Fries* may be obtained by contacting the publisher, History is a Hoot, Inc., P.O. Box 285, Markham, Virginia 22643-0285; telephone (540) 622-2074. Quantity discounts are available. Please see order form in back for more information.

Table of Contents

ACKNOWLEDGMENTS

INSPIRATION for *Spies, Pop Flies, and French Fries* came from the thousands of young people with whom I have had the fun and privilege of sharing stories about some of our nation's lesser known heroes and heroines. Happily for me, to several of these up and coming history buffs and preservationists, I am an aunt, a godmother, or a friend. They are: Baby Boy Blake, Kelly Fuksa, Kristi Fuksa, Amy Johnson, Ryan Johnson, Virginia Johnson, Billy McCarthy, Brian McCarthy, Joseph McCarthy, Matthew McCarthy, Rory McCarthy, Tassos McCarthy, Daniel Randlett, John Hunter Rankin, Chris Ridings, Steve Ridings, Jeff Sholes, and Tracy Sholes.

For their assistance and encouragement while I was writing this book, my profound gratitude goes to a number of special individuals: Louise Abbruzzese, Willie Banks, Patricia Blake, Paul Blake, Michael Bohumil, Dede Bonner, Elizabeth Bruins, Lorna Catling, Tom Crouch, René J. Défourneaux, David Donovan, Chuck Evans, Kathy Evans, Dan Ford, Edwin J. Ford, Jr., Edward Goldman, Von Hardesty, Catherine Devine Hayden, Richard Johnson, Teresa Johnson, Stanley Lawson, Mary Matteo, David McCarthy, Gia McCarthy, Josephine McCarthy, Lauren McCarthy, William McCarthy, Elizabeth McIntosh, James Parks, Kathleen Parks, Laura Putnam, Carol Randlett, Randy Randlett, Betty Rankin, Joanne Ridings, Kristen Sanders, Elizabeth Shames, Judith Sholes, Dolores Smerz, Annie Snyder, Diane Studeman, Mary Triarhos, and Joyce Zerbe.

For their considerable proofing skills, I am especially indebted to three gifted editors: Gemma R. Dehnbostel, Patricia A. Fuksa, and Anne B. McDonald. All were exceptionally generous with their time, talent, and friendship.

Finally, to Nick Crettier, the accomplished photographer who converted an eclectic collection of slides, negatives, transparencies, and pictures into the illustrations reproduced in this book, a Shenandoah Valley "huzzah" for his good work and considerable patience.

To each and all, I offer a sincere and heartfelt "thank you" for your belief in me and in this endeavor.

INTRODUCTION

You Ought to Write a Book

OF the several challenging assignments I enjoyed during my 24 years with the Central Intelligence Agency, none was as professionally and personally rewarding as my final position. For nine years, I supervised the CIA Exhibit Center, a collection of espionage memorabilia housed in the Agency's Headquarters building in Langley, Virginia. Highlighting this experience were the tours my assistants and I conducted for hundreds of special visitors who requested guided walk-throughs of the Center during their visit to the CIA. Granted limited access to the secured compound as official guests of the Agency, this list of VIPs included symposium participants, media representatives, heads of foreign countries, entertainment and sports celebrities, and U.S. government and private-sector leaders.

While it was always exciting to meet these notable individuals and share with them the different items that made up the Center's unique collection, my real thrill as curator came from hosting tours comprised principally of young people and their parents and teachers. As odd as it may seem, there were quite a few such groups, representing a variety of social, cultural, and educational institutions nationwide. This influx resulted from the Agency's attempt to expand its outreach effort, which began in earnest during the early 1990s.

One such initiative involved Westinghouse Science Fair winners from the District of Columbia, Maryland, Virginia, and West Virginia. On a given Saturday each May, hundreds of bright and engaging high school students visited the Exhibit Center as part of their day at the CIA. These young men and women brought with them an enthusiasm that was palpable and contagious. Leaning on every word, they offered questions and insights overlooked by most adults, including the collection's curator. Following the tour, many of the students asked for the names of books that could provide more information about the topics we had covered. These requests were especially gratifying. Also heartening was the interest shown by the parents and teachers. They were active participants in this invigorating learning process. It was hard to tell sometimes who enjoyed the journey more, the high schoolers or the adults.

Then there was the emotional hour spent with the Make-A-Wish Foundation children. Representatives from the organization would contact the Agency when an acutely ill child had but one wish—to be a spy. During their VIP tour of the Headquarters compound, these inspiring kids were treated to demonstrations by bomb sniffing dogs and to briefings by technicians who develop gadgets similar to those made famous in the James Bond movies. Sometime during a day that was dictated by the children's preferences and condition, the Exhibit Center was also visited. As they handled some of the smaller artifacts, their eyes grew wide with pure excitement and joy. It was a look that stayed with us and served as a reminder of how indomitable the human spirit really is. We were enriched by these visits more than the child or the family could ever know.

The accounts in this book grew out of the monologues I gave to the many guests—young and young at heart—who toured the CIA Exhibit Center. Espionage seemed to be an inherently appealing topic for visitors, no matter their age or gender. Always a favorite were the stories concerning Maj. Gen. William J. Donovan's legendary World War II-era Office of Strategic Services (OSS) and its present-day successor, the Central Intelligence Agency. When stories of operations and operatives were combined with demonstrations using some of the tools of the trade, the interest level intensified even more. This was especially true of the school-aged visitors. Students of all backgrounds and grade levels eagerly crowded around an exhibit case, hoping for a closer look or even a chance to hold some of the "spy toys."

More than once during my tenure as the Center's first curator I heard, "You ought to write a book." So I did. It is designed to mirror the subjects of the guided tours I gave to my favorite visitors—the young people. (Because all were extemporaneous and customized to fit the interest of a particular individual or group, there are no formal written transcripts of the presentations.)

In the "Operation Explore More" section at the end of each chapter and in most of the "Name That HUMINT" answers, I have tried to include sources to help readers undertake their own intelligence-gathering missions targeting some of the subjects presented in *Spies, Pop Flies, and French Fries.* Everyone is cleared for these operations.

My wish is that this book be both fun and educational. It is affectionately dedicated with great respect to those who serve and to those who learn.

Linda McCarthy
January 1999

The CIA Exhibit Center as it appeared in early 1997. All of the artifacts displayed in the 1,400-square-foot facility were gifted to the collection, usually by the individual or group who designed or used a particular item. *Courtesy CIA Exhibit Center.*

Author and founding curator of the CIA Exhibit Center Linda McCarthy (right) with World War II veteran William H. Pietsch. A decorated member of an elite OSS Jedburgh (special forces) team, Colonel Pietsch loaned some of his personal memorabilia to the Center for display. *Courtesy Central Intelligence Agency.*

CHAPTER ONE

Signals and Signs

WHILE I was curator of the CIA Exhibit Center, several reproductions of period photographs hung on an entryway wall, the display suggesting something of the local area's—and the Agency's—rich Civil War heritage. One of these images showed a U.S. Army signal tower erected at Chain Bridge, a vital transportation link to the Federal City that spanned the Potomac River. Thousands of vehicles weekly cross the modern-day version of this bridge, which is located just down the road from CIA Headquarters. Sadly, nothing remains of the overhead observation and communications post that helped protect the District of Columbia during the Civil War.

A busy facility in its day, the lookout point was vital to the security of wartime Washington. Situated near Georgetown and its commercial port, the installation's significance grew as hostilities between North and South became more frequent and ever bloodier. Moreover, the tower's presence was as symbolic as it was strategic: it not only stood a quick horseback ride from President Abraham Lincoln's White House, but it also provided a commanding view of the Potomac. An important lifeline to Washington, the waterway formed a natural and ideological border separating the Union capital from one of the Confederacy's most powerful states—Virginia.

Gathering and transmitting information is a large part of what the CIA does. The Exhibit Center photograph helped illustrate the historical ties between signal stations of the 1860s and today's technologically advanced systems guarding America as an anxious world strives to confront the challenges of a new millennium.

Present-day intelligence lexicon (or "spook-speak") features a host of specially coined words that reflect the far-reaching ways information is obtained. Some examples are: ELINT (electronic intelligence); IMINT (imagery intelligence); RADINT (radar intelligence); COMINT (communications intelligence); and LASINT (laser intelligence). There are many more, and all underscore the diverse methods employed to gather intelligence, whatever its origin.

In this alphabet soup of acronyms, two of the principal spook-speak terms are SIGINT (signals intelligence) and HUMINT (human intelligence). Both are very important sources of information that help keep our nation's leaders apprised of a variety of potential threats. Today, these dangers can include anything from actual armed military aggression to the growing menace of international terrorism. HUMINT, of course, involves information gleaned from individuals, often called assets. SIGINT is a more modern concept that encompasses a range of intercepted communications—everything from satellite transmissions to telephone taps. (ELINT, IMINT, RADINT, COMINT, and LASINT are related to SIGINT.) Two extremely critical intelligence-gathering techniques, HUMINT and especially SIGINT, can trace at least part of their ancestry back to the Civil War-era stations and the courageous officers and enlisted personnel of both the Union and Confederate Signal Corps who served atop them.

Considered noncombatants, these aerial scouts carried no real weapons, despite often being used for recreational target practice by an adversary. Compounding matters was the constant threat posed to them by serious snipers and artillerymen from the opposing side who had orders to take out the elevated eavesdroppers as a matter of military policy. But the signalmen persevered, peering through telescopes to the ground below for anything that could create difficulties for their army. Besides monitoring enemy troop positions, the lookouts kept a keen eye out for recent alterations made by man or nature to the surrounding landscape, particularly transportation routes. In today's spook-speak, these observations are known as change detection. Such information was especially critical to Civil War units, which moved primarily on foot. For instance, a bridge washed from a creek swollen by flash flooding might have to be replaced by members of the Engineer Corps before infantry regiments resumed their march to the next battle site. When the signalmen saw a potential problem, they hurriedly let their commanders on the ground know about it, providing what is now called HUMINT.

Besides serving as overhead reconnaissance positions, these stations also functioned as message relay and reception platforms for a type of military communications used extensively throughout the war by each side. Formally labeled aerial telegraphy, the method was commonly referred to as the wigwag system. Looking closely at the picture of the Chain Bridge tower, the distinctive piece of equipment responsible for the popular nickname could barely be seen to the top left. It was a specially designed signal flag, all but a hint of it lost on the image because 19th-century cameras could not capture moving subjects, including cloth banners flapping in a stiff wind. Since wigwagging relied upon a series of precise and prescribed flag movements and positions to transmit messages, Civil War-era photographers probably never recorded an actual instance where it was used. (Nevertheless, some of the more creative and enterprising cameramen following the armies around may have staged the event, as they routinely did a variety of combat and camp scenes.)

You might recognize these flags from books or even from old movies. Most were white with a large red square in the middle. To improve visibility against snowscapes or the sky, signalmen generally used black flags with white centers. For mixed backdrops like cities or harbors, red flags with white middle squares stood out better. Torches and lanterns were preferred for nighttime transmissions.

In and around a theater of operations that was especially important, such as Washington, D.C., or the fertile Shenandoah Valley of Virginia, a string of elevated observation and communications platforms would be manned by experienced signalmen, who systemically wigwagged messages from post to post until they reached their destination. Across the mountain tops overlooking the Valley, signal stations dotted the length of the 140-mile-long "Granary of the Confederacy." While one side may have constructed and initially occupied a certain site, control of these vital intelligence links shifted with the fluid war situation. Consequently, stations that facilitated Stonewall Jackson's famed Valley Campaign of 1862 would later be in the hands of Union signalmen after Philip Sheridan's Army of the Shenandoah finally drove the Southerners from their breadbasket during the fall of 1864.

As use of the wigwag system expanded to include most major battle venues, military leaders were determined to protect their communications as much as possible. Waved from hilltop to hilltop, there was always the very real chance these transmissions might be seen and recorded by those with a strong spyglass and a trained eye. Both armies used cipher disks to disguise and protect messages; the Federals deemed the encrypting devices so vital to field operations that soldiers were urged to sacrifice their own lives to ensure the security of the brass wheels. It was not until after radios and teletypes were introduced into combat during the next century that the practice whereby Northern and Southern signalmen intercepted each other's transmissions became known as SIGINT.

The influence of Civil War-era SIGINT techniques has transcended time and new technologies, helping to safeguard sophisticated communications systems—both Earth and space-based—that the Yankee and Rebel flagmen perched in trees and on rooftops could never have imagined. Recalling the use of cipher disks, today's transmissions are routinely encrypted to protect them from SIGINT snooping. And, just as the signalmen relayed false intelligence at times to misdirect or confuse their counterparts, modern cryptographers also include fabricated data in electronic transmissions for the same purpose. In present-day spook-speak, this bogus information is called deception material.

Officially adopted by the U.S. government barely one year before the fall of Fort Sumter, the wigwag system proved especially useful to commanders trying to organize and orchestrate battles where telegraph lines had been cut or never strung. Its inventor was a bright and dedicated Army surgeon who had worked as a telegrapher while attending Buffalo Medical College. Albert J. Myer was a man of many interests, including art and the evolving science of meteorology. He was especially intrigued by the different manual communication methods employed by the deaf populations of the era; Myer's extensive research on the topic became the basis for a required medical school thesis. In the paper, Myer outlined a new manual language for the deaf he had devised whereby individuals would gently fingerspell words on each other's faces and hands using an alphabet based on codes developed to relay messages telegraphically.

After joining the Army in 1854 as an assistant surgeon, the freshly commissioned lieutenant was ordered to the New Mexico Territory. Like most, he soon grew frustrated with the length of time it took to send dispatches by mounted courier across the vast Western frontier. Determined to create an inexpensive, reliable, and portable message transmission system for the military, Myer began culling the different communication methods he had documented over the years. He then set about creating what would become known as the wigwag system.

First there was the matter of an alphabet. As he had with his manual alphabet for the deaf, the former telegraph operator turned to the popular (and competing) Bain and Morse codes and their underlying precept that letters can be numerically represented—whether by dots and dashes or fingers or flags. While not unknown to the Army, use of these codes in regions like the Great Plains was necessarily limited: there simply were not enough poles, wires, and stations in place to move messages electrically over telegraph lines. But Myer believed information could be conveyed manually across immense distances, precluding the need for an elaborate and expensive transmission and reception network. It was his comprehensive study of the various communication methods used by deaf people that had repeatedly proved to him the merit and practicality of manual languages.

For a mode of delivery, Myer had to look no further than the bluffs ringing the different Army posts. There, time and again, he had witnessed Comanche braves signaling to each other with their spears from prominent ridges.

If the deaf, Myer reasoned, could communicate utilizing an accepted pattern of finger placements derived from telegraphers' codes, why couldn't the Army send messages incorporating these same codes and then relay them by way of flags, as the Comanches had gestured their intentions from butte to butte with spears? Presented to Congress in 1859, Albert J. Myer's newly patented aerial telegraphy was an ingeniously crafted combination of all these elements.

On a few occasions, students from nearby schools for the deaf were guests in the Exhibit Center. When these visitors learned the role that manual communication played in the evolution of Civil War-era message transmission, a justified pride was evident in their broad smiles.

While relating this story to the many hearing guests who toured the Center, I often used elements of American Sign Language to make the narrative more visible and memorable. The youngest visitors seemed to remember best those signs associated with fast food. One popular example was French fries, the sign for which is quickly and easily learned and replicated. With the dominant hand held straight up (and palm facing out), the ends of the thumb and forefinger are joined, leaving the remaining three fingers grouped together. This is the letter "f" in the modern manual alphabet, which has as part of its historical legacy the manual alphabet Albert Myer devised using telegraph codes. When repeated twice (f f), it becomes the sign for French fries.

As this discussion of HUMINT, history, SIGINT, and signs wound down, another kind of "wigwagging" often emerged. After filing past the picture of the Chain Bridge tower and out the Exhibit Center door, many youngsters could be seen practicing the sign for French fries as they walked through the long hallways at CIA Headquarters. Watching these rapid hand and arm movements slowly disappear down the corridors, I was reminded of the Civil War signalmen. There was this satisfying sense that Major Myer and the aerial telegraphers from both sides would have dipped their flags in approval.

Many Civil War battle re-creations throughout the country include wigwag demonstrations by knowledgeable and authentic Signal Corps reenactors. One of the best ways to find out about upcoming events near you is to subscribe to the *Civil War News.* Printed monthly in Vermont, the periodical, in addition to numerous articles, publishes a current listing of Civil War-related activities across the nation. Call 1 (800) 222-1861, and the good people at the *News* will send a free introductory copy to get you started.

Visit the U.S. Army Signal Corps Museum, either in person or via the Internet, for an absorbing look at the history of the Signal Corps. Located on the grounds of Fort Gordon, Georgia, the actual facility features a collection of more than 10,000 objects. (Many of Albert Myer's personal artifacts are displayed here.) Managed by a very helpful and knowledgeable staff, the museum is a fascinating place to explore the evolution of modern signal communications.

To learn more about the deaf and their heritage, Gallaudet University, the world's only university for deaf and hard-of-hearing undergraduate students, provides an array of resources. Among other things, the school, which is located in Washington, D.C., publishes a catalogue featuring a wide range of books and gift items relating to deaf culture. Look for the Gallaudet home page on the Internet.

Photograph that hung in the CIA Exhibit Center of the Chain Bridge signal tower. Part of the defensive perimeter that safeguarded Washington during the Civil War, the station stood in the vicinity of the Signal Corps training camp established by the Federal Army near the campus of Georgetown College (now University). *Courtesy U.S. Army Military History Institute, Carlisle, Pennsylvania.*

Wartime image of Chain Bridge. Situated not far from where the English explorer and colonist Capt. John Smith visited in 1608, an earlier version of this Potomac overpass was built as a suspension bridge that required a system of chains to raise and lower it. Although succeeding structures have been constructed from a variety of materials, the designation Chain Bridge remains. *Courtesy Library of Congress (LC-B 8184-7657), with special thanks to Mary Ison.*

Modern-day U.S. Army Signal Corps regimental crest featuring a Civil War-era signal flag. The Latin motto is translated as "Watchful for the country." *Courtesy U.S. Army Signal Corps Museum, Fort Gordon, Georgia, with special thanks to Mike Rodgers.*

Confederate signal station at Beverly's Ford in Virginia. Reproduced from a wartime wood engraving, this image depicts a Rebel observation and communications post situated near Brandy Station. On June 9, 1863, the fields surrounding the Culpeper County railroad hamlet became the site of the largest cavalry battle ever fought in the Western Hemisphere—the day-long Battle of Brandy Station. One of the objectives of lookout positions such as this was to help protect important transportation routes like rail lines. *Author's collection.*

Brig. Gen. Albert J. Myer. In addition to his pioneering work as the first chief of the Union Signal Corps, Myer is credited with helping to establish in 1870 what is known today as the National Weather Service. Fort Myer, located next to Arlington National Cemetery in Northern Virginia, is named for this soldier-scientist. *Author's collection.*

CHAPTER TWO

Sky-High Spies

DISPLAYED on the same Exhibit Center wall as the Chain Bridge signal tower image was another black and white photograph, this one reflecting something of America's first brushes with what is known in modern-day spook-speak as aerial reconnaissance. It showed Professor Thaddeus Lowe's gas-generating wagons situated near an unfinished Capitol dome. Technological marvels for the time, these specially designed rigs were waiting to fill one of eight observation balloons that the scientific visionary from New Hampshire would eventually fly during the first two years of the Civil War to gather information for the Union Army. The CIA Headquarters building now stands just a 20-minute drive from the site where Professor Lowe first floated aloft in his tethered aerostat *Enterprise* to demonstrate the military applications of aerial surveillance to Abraham Lincoln. Inside this striking concrete, glass, and metal structure, analysts examine data obtained from today's high-resolution satellites.

Underscoring the Agency's involvement in the development and utilization of these silent sentinels is the now declassified CORONA project, considered America's first satellite program. A working model of CORONA's panoramic camera became part of the Exhibit Center's collection for a time. During its stay, the model sat near the wall where the image illustrating Professor Lowe's attempts at aerial reconnaissance hung. While we would like to claim this historical twist was planned, we can't. The satellite camera was moved there in February 1994 to await transfer to its final destination—a permanent home in the Smithsonian Institution's National Air and Space Museum in Washington, D.C. One year later, the camera model, along with copies of CORONA's first declassified images, was formally presented to the Smithsonian during a ceremony at CIA Headquarters. With the unveiling of the "Space Race" exhibit at the Air and Space Museum in May 1997, people from all over the United States and the world could finally view the CORONA camera. Displayed around the model, which measures as long as a full-size automobile, is an impressive array of Soviet and American satellite hardware that worked to keep a fragile peace during the Cold War.

Publicly labeled the DISCOVERER Program, some CORONA missions did have a secondary biomedical research role. This helped support, if only for awhile, official pronouncements that the U.S. was embarking on a study of environmental conditions in space. (Laboratory mice were actually included on one flight as part of a scientific payload.) Whatever the cover name and story, the primary objective of CORONA and its revolutionary stereo-optical photographic system was overhead photo reconnaissance of the former Soviet Union and mainland China. While some of CORONA's photographs by today's standards could be considered grainy, they still gave the United States a revealing and expansive look at these powerful allies during the height of the nuclear arms race. From August 1960 to May 1972, CORONA imagery told American civilian and military leaders much about the strength and location of Soviet and Chinese troops; the numerous shipyards, submarine bases, and airfields built and operated by the two secretive Communist nations were also monitored. Of special interest were Soviet intercontinental ballistic missile sites and the threat they posed to the Free World.

Beyond the concerns and challenges of the Cold War, many of the technological advances originally developed for CORONA missions later benefited America's manned space program. Photographic techniques introduced during CORONA surveillance flights were adapted by engineers designing imaging equipment for the Apollo project. Another important contribution evolved from CORONA's revolutionary rocket steering feature. NASA refined the innovation for use on its coming fleet of space shuttle orbiters, allowing the crafts greater maneuvering and docking ability.

With the official release of the CORONA story in 1995, another important aspect of the program emerged. Not only do reels upon reels of its imagery show various military complexes, but they also detail other significant features of the landscape below—many of them natural and some adversely affected by man-made factors. It is these photographs that have agriculturists, arborists, botanists, environmentalists, geologists, hydrologists, and zoologists so excited. Twelve years of CORONA flights, which provided photographic coverage of approximately 750,000,000 square nautical miles of the Earth's surface, have produced a permanent record that will be used to detect and monitor changes in the world's ecosystems. When examined by scientists, these graphics can pinpoint concerns such as deforestation and desertification, as well as coastline erosion and wetlands degradation.

Underscoring this is one of CORONA's early images—a 1962 photograph of the Aral Sea located on the border of Kazakhstan and Uzbekistan. When placed next to an August 1994 photo of this region taken from a NOAA satellite, the effects of redirecting too much water for irrigation are dramatically illustrated. Experts estimate the Aral Sea has lost a volume of water equal to one and a half times that of Lake Erie during the last 30 years. These two pictures displayed side by side proved it. As more of CORONA's imagery is declassified and released, environmentalists from all over the world will have photographic evidence of other ecological problem sites. Scientists anticipate such knowledge will be used in the future to document these areas, increasing the odds that, whatever the past harm done to the land or those populating it, the damage can be studied and possibly even reversed.

This concept has been expanded to include imagery from today's spies-in-the-sky now orbiting the Earth. American satellites that routinely target such trouble spots as the Middle East and Bosnia can be programmed, once a detailed and thorough administrative and legal process has been completed, to photograph such life-threatening natural disasters as floods, hurricanes, and earthquakes occurring in our own country. With the high-resolution pictures supplied by these systems, rescue workers can be sent to where they are most needed, whether it is into a region of rising flood waters or back to a redeveloping hot spot in a forest fire.

Image-processing technologies developed for national defense purposes are also being adapted for medical science, enhancing opportunities for saving and enriching lives. Clinicians, for instance, believe that satellite-imaging techniques designed to locate Scud missiles during the Persian Gulf war can improve a woman's chances against breast cancer. With digital mammography, radiologists are optimistic they will be able to detect subtle tissue changes and hidden cancerous growths not always revealed by standard methods.

As the "Father of American Aerial Reconnaissance" and as a scientist, Professor Lowe would be pleased the discoveries he pioneered for the Union war effort over 135 years ago are the basis for the technological advances of today that protect not only the nation's security, but also the welfare of its people. As keepers of the CORONA camera for more than a year, those of us responsible for the Exhibit Center collection also experienced a sense of personal satisfaction. We enjoyed caring for the model and sharing the story of our nation's first satellite program with the many visitors who came to view the one-of-a-kind piece of Cold War memorabilia while it was displayed at the Agency.

Following the camera's relocation to the Smithsonian, we enlarged a color picture taken of the artifact when it was still featured at CIA Headquarters. Alongside reproductions of the first declassified CORONA images, we hung the oversize graphic on a wall in the Exhibit Center near where the camera itself had rested. Coupled with the photograph showing Professor Lowe's ballooning equipment parked on what is now the National Mall, these depictions of 20th-century overhead reconnaissance told something of space exploration's historic beginnings and the contribution of America's sky-high spies to that epic effort.

Operation Explore More

For more information about Civil War aerial reconnaissance and Professor Lowe, a good start is *The Eagle Aloft: Two Centuries of the Balloon in America,* published in 1983 by the Smithsonian Institution Press. Author Tom Crouch devoted nearly 80 pages of this 770-page volume to Civil War ballooning.

To learn more about the historic CORONA program and other space-based espionage systems, beg, borrow, but don't steal copies of the various and assorted videos produced by the Discovery Channel that explore this fascinating topic. Click on the company's Web site to find out about the availability of these popular presentations, most of which are drawn from previously aired Discovery Channel programs.

For those who want the official word on CORONA, you can purchase a bound copy of the project's original declassified government documents from the National Technical Information Service in Springfield, Virginia. Telephone orders can be placed by calling 1 (800) 553-NTIS. A nice operator will ask for the title of the item you are seeking. In this case it is: *CORONA: America's First Satellite Program.* One in a series of published CIA Cold War records, the book costs about $80 but is well edited and readable.

As for the actual model of the CORONA camera, you and your family can visit it in person at the National Air and Space Museum. A featured attraction in the highly acclaimed "Space Race" exhibit, the camera looks out across the grounds where Professor Lowe, hovering in the *Enterprise,* convinced President Lincoln during the early days of the Civil War that aerial reconnaissance could play an important role in the nation's security. The Air and Space Museum maintains a wonderful Web site. Check it out for details about the "Space Race" display, as well as other attractions filling the galleries of America's most popular museum.

Photograph that hung in the CIA Exhibit Center showing Professor Thaddeus Lowe's gas-generating wagons near the U.S. Capitol. Each rig carried an 11-foot tank into which iron filings were distributed. Sulfuric acid was poured over the filings, creating hydrogen. After undergoing a cooling and purification process, the gas was pumped into the waiting aerostat. Another way Professor Lowe inflated his balloon *Enterprise* while visiting the Federal City in 1861 was by simply tapping into a Washington Gas Company main. *Courtesy National Archives (16-AD-2).*

Professor Lowe's aerostat *Intrepid* in the spring of 1862 during Gen. George McClellan's Peninsula Campaign to capture the Confederate capital of Richmond. In large part because of information obtained from the aeronaut's tethered ascents, the Union Army enjoyed a tactical victory at the Battle of Fair Oaks or Seven Pines. *Courtesy Library of Congress (LC-B 8171-2349), with special thanks to Mary Ison.*

CORONA camera model at CIA Headquarters. Launched aboard a Thor booster, the Agena spacecraft housing CORONA's panoramic camera system did not return to Earth. Once a mission was completed, the nose cone containing the expended spools of film was jettisoned for midair capture by Air Force crews flying planes equipped with an apparatus that snagged the capsule's parachute before the recovery vehicle landed in the Pacific. Pictured sitting in front of the model is the last film-return bucket retrieved from outer space when the 12-year program ended May 25, 1972. Twenty-five years later, both artifacts became part of the "Space Race" exhibit at the National Air and Space Museum in Washington, D.C. *Courtesy CIA Exhibit Center.*

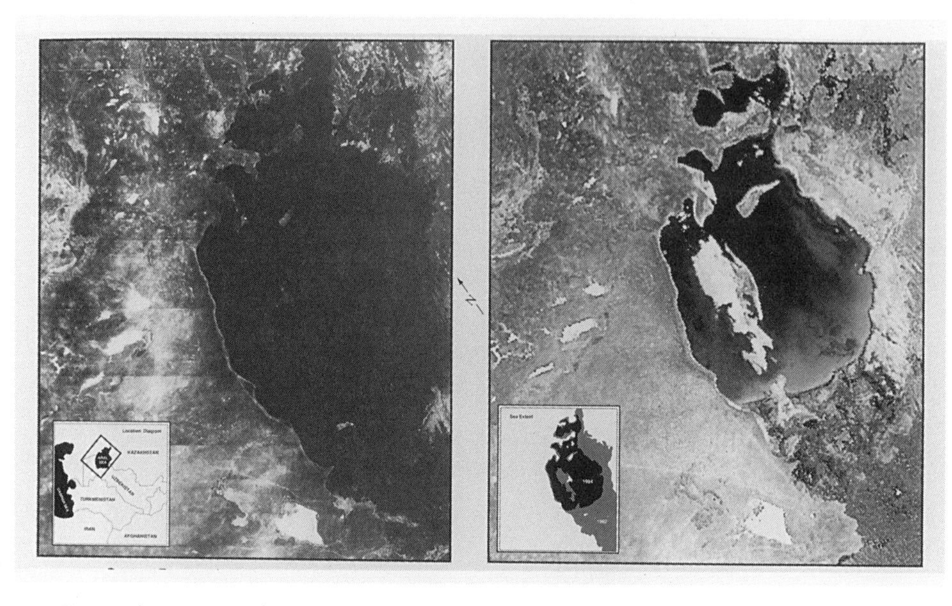

Reproduction of a government-produced handout incorporating CORONA (left) and National Oceanic and Atmospheric Administration (NOAA) satellite pictures that shows three decades of ecological damage to the Aral Sea. (The ancient body of water is represented by the black spot to the right in each photograph.) Space-based photo reconnaissance systems are now routinely used in a variety of ways to document conditions negatively impacting the Earth's environment. Urban planners, for instance, can chart the effects of uncontrolled sprawl on a particular region with imagery obtained from satellites. *Courtesy Central Intelligence Agency.*

CHAPTER THREE

Fighting Bandits and Bigotry

ONE of the aside stories I liked to tell during guided walk-throughs of the Exhibit Center concerned the Buffalo Soldiers—particularly the African American horsemen of the Old West who distinguished themselves as members of the all-black 9th and 10th U.S. Cavalry Regiments. Regrettably, the Center had no artifacts linked to these intrepid troopers. Usually talks about the Buffalo Soldiers entered a tour monologue as part of a "Name That HUMINT" segment. Those of you who read the chapter titled "Signals and Signs" know about HUMINT, which stands for human intelligence, or information obtained from individuals.

With my "Name That HUMINT" trivia time, I would take a break from the standard tour and toss out a question concerning some of the lesser known aspects of American history that are also—wait for it—*interesting*. Often these surprise topics only remotely resembled what was being discussed at a particular display. Some visitors labeled the digression a pop quiz. Not quite. My little game was nonthreatening, and no school I knew ever required a correct response as part of its graduation prerequisite. If any human in the group (including teachers and chaperons) gave the right answer (intelligence data), he or she was rewarded with a chance to don the curator's protective white gloves and hold one of the treasures from whatever case was being featured at the time.

To be sure, I could make the rest of the group just a little nervous by allowing this junior James Bond the opportunity to handle an actual item of tradecraft, which is simply a spook-speak term for the various methods and tools used by intelligence organizations around the globe to gather information and manage clandestine operations. The World War II-era tire-puncturing caltrop was always a hit; so, too, were some of the miniature cameras on display in what I called the "gotcha case." Sadly, questions about the Buffalo Soldiers rarely resulted in such a prize. They did, however, serve as a springboard to an impromptu verbal account of the black soldiers who helped settle the American frontier between 1866 and the advent of the 20th century.

Most of the troopers chosen for the 9th and 10th Cavalry units (and for what evolved into the all-black 24th and 25th U.S. Infantry Regiments, as well) were veterans of the Civil War. Following President Lincoln's Emancipation Proclamation, the Union Army, whose need for willing and able volunteers had become acute from two years of bloody fighting, began to actively recruit blacks. Officially designated the U.S. Colored Troops in May 1863, these segregated regiments were almost always commanded by white officers. (Pressing manpower shortages also compelled the Confederate Congress to pass a law shortly before the fall of Richmond permitting blacks to join the Southern army as combatants.) When Lee met Grant at Appomattox on Palm Sunday 1865 to discuss the terms of surrender, nearly 200,000 African Americans had seen service with the Federal Army and Navy.

A few narratives have been written focusing on these brave men who fought for liberty and a united America; some of the more outstanding depictions can be found in the memoirs of the great abolitionist, Frederick Douglass. As a rule, however, the African American Civil War soldiers' legacy was largely bypassed in books until only recently. Films portraying their valor and sacrifice were even more scarce. Hollywood finally offered an inspiring look at one unit, the 54th Massachusetts Infantry, in the widely acclaimed 1989 movie, *Glory*.

Beyond these notable exceptions, much about the black contribution to our nation's armed conflicts, including the 5,000 African Americans who served in the Revolutionary War, had been forgotten. This was especially true of the Buffalo Soldiers.

Not particularly welcome at Army forts in the East, black enlistees were sent to man outposts springing up across the burgeoning American West—desolate installations that sometimes resembled ramshackle ghost towns more than military bases. Worse still were the deplorable sanitary conditions. Diseases like cholera and tuberculosis spread uncontrollably throughout the sites, claiming both military and civilian casualties.

Beyond the campgrounds, more adversity awaited. Life on the frontier could be harsh and exacting, no matter a soldier's color. Weather extremes presented some of the most demanding challenges. Winter in the Northern Great Plains meant wild and frigid winds cutting through rider and horse alike. Summers in the Southwest were punctuated by a piercing, draining sun that beat down on a dusty landscape barely fit for scorpions and rattlesnakes. Added to these ordeals were the substandard provisions and mounts often issued to the all-black regiments, with the better horses, equipment, and food earmarked for the established eastern posts. More often than not, the Buffalo Soldiers took the inferior leather goods and reworked and polished them to a high sheen that reflected not only a regiment's pride, but also its resolve. Rotting rations were replaced by wild game the men hunted and then cooked over a warm and welcoming campfire. Guided by their determination and resourcefulness, the black troopers forged themselves into superior fighting units that recorded less desertions and more reenlistments than white regiments. Moreover, many Buffalo Soldiers received decorations for bravery, including the Medal of Honor.

Besides acts of institutional discrimination directed at them by Army commanders and Washington bureaucrats, the Buffalo Soldiers were confronted with a more personal kind of prejudice as they helped protect migrating Americans and immigrating foreigners making their way west. A number of settlers were recently defeated Confederates who brought with them the same tightly held attitudes and beliefs that helped sustain four years of civil war between North and South. These sentiments were sometimes softened when the new residents witnessed firsthand the valor, dedication, and professionalism exhibited by the all-black units who had been dispatched to protect the transplanted Southerners and their property.

The Cheyenne and Comanches also came to greatly respect the black cavalrymen, calling them Buffalo Soldiers as a matter of honor and esteem. To these proud Native American tribes, the troopers' woolly hair resembled the hide of the mighty and revered bovine that roamed the Plains, providing the indigenous peoples with an abundant source of food and clothing.

While their heroic deeds went largely unheralded at the time, one observer of note did chronicle some of the Buffalo Soldiers' trials and triumphs. Long recognized for his paintings and sculptures depicting life on the Western frontier, Frederic Remington became a champion of the African American units, documenting in both words and drawings some of what they experienced and achieved. Riding with the cavalrymen on scouting patrols and living with them in dismal and confining forts, Remington sketched and wrote a number of accounts that provided a revealing look at something of what the stoic and resolute troopers had endured.

Despite their many travails, the Buffalo Soldiers managed to help tame a vast and unforgiving land. When not fighting Mexican revolutionaries, cattle rustlers, or hostile Indians, these men, especially those from the 24th and 25th Infantry Regiments, performed backbreaking fatigue duty. Besides building and rebuilding Army posts, the all-black units constructed critical roadways and bridges throughout the region. Buffalo Soldiers also strung miles of telegraph line needed to speed communications between the growing number of settlements. Perhaps most important, the cavalrymen were pathfinders, exploring and mapping thousands of acres of uncharted territory, greatly facilitating America's westward movement.

Continuing this tradition of service, elements of the Buffalo Soldiers participated in every major conflict of the 20th century up to and including the Korean war. The 3rd Battalion of the all-black 24th Infantry Regiment now is credited with one of the first successful battles fought by United Nations forces on the contested Korean peninsula. Nearly 40 years after the unit's courageous stand at Yechon in 1950, the U.S. government, in an official study commissioned by the Secretary of the Army, formally acknowledged the outstanding devotion to duty exhibited by these Buffalo Soldiers.

In 1992, a monument honoring the original Buffalo Soldiers was dedicated at Fort Leavenworth, Kansas, where the 10th Cavalry had been formed 126 years earlier. In the crowd were several younger Buffalo Soldiers who had remained in the military after the different branches were eventually integrated following President Harry Truman's executive order of 1948. Delivering the keynote address at the ceremony was Army Gen. Colin Powell, who told the audience, "We are not here to criticize an America of 150 years ago, but to rejoice that we live in a country that has permitted a spiritual descendant of the Buffalo Soldiers to stand before you today as the first African American chairman of the Joint Chiefs of Staff. I am deeply mindful of the debt I owe to those who went before me . . . I will never forget their service and their sacrifice."

As I ended this edition of "Name That HUMINT," at least one member of the visiting group would remark, "I never heard of these soldiers."

Why did I focus part of my study and tour talks on a topic for which the Center had no artifact to display? I could make the case that the black cavalry troopers of the Old West often operated as scouts and couriers, gathering and relaying information about threats facing military installations and emerging population centers. But the answer was really much simpler. The Buffalo Soldiers interested me as an individual and as an American.

One of the most acknowledged books about the African American regiments is *The Buffalo Soldiers: A Narrative of the Negro Cavalry in the West* by William H. Leckie and published in 1967. While somewhat dated, it still provides one of the best overall insights into the black troopers who played such an important role in the settlement of the Western frontier.

If you are interested in learning more about the American artist who recorded something of the Buffalo Soldiers' accomplishments and courage, consider a visit to the Frederic Remington Art Museum in Ogdensburg, New York. Here the whole story of this talented man is depicted. Reproductions of some of his more famous prints and sculptures can be purchased from the museum shop, as can a copy of William Leckie's book. Contact the friendly staff by phoning (315) 393-2425 or check the museum's home page on the Internet.

For a truly inspirational and memorable look at the life of the fabled black cavalrymen, try to locate an appearance by a unit of Buffalo Soldiers reenactors made up of young people from the VisionQuest organization. A national group dedicated to reaching troubled teenagers, VisionQuest established its Buffalo Soldiers program in 1977. Stressing "heritage as treatment," the project incorporates traditional academics with physically demanding military training. Assisting the professional staff in this important work are actual Buffalo Soldier veterans of World War II and Korea, who offer their experiences and expertise to these adolescents, helping them realize their full potential and become model citizens.

Once the VisionQuest "recruits" complete an intensive training period (including practice sessions to master the same intricate mounted drills executed by the original Buffalo Soldiers), the young troopers perform at a variety of community events across the country, such as holiday parades. In addition, graduates appear before school assemblies, encouraging students to further their education and to avoid drugs and alcohol. With authentically reproduced uniforms and atop well conditioned horses, these impressive young Americans continue the noble tradition of the black cavalry trooper. For a schedule of their coming appearances, contact VisionQuest National, Ltd., P.O. Box 12906, Tucson, Arizona 85732, or check the VisionQuest home page on the Internet.

An invaluable resource for a wide range of black history topics, including the Buffalo Soldiers, is the Web site maintained by Bennie J. McRae of *Lest We Forget.* The information presented here is incredible. Take advantage of these authoritative accounts that are as entertaining as they are educational. Also included is an updated listing of reenactments that feature living historians portraying not only Buffalo Soldiers, but also other inspirational African Americans such as the men of the 54th Massachusetts Infantry Regiment depicted in the movie *Glory.* This fascinating computer link also examines the important role played by black women throughout American history. Do yourself (and your next term paper) a favor by checking out *Lest We Forget* and all that it offers. You will not be disappointed.

As for the U.S. Colored Troops who served during the Civil War, they are now receiving some of the recognition long overdue them. Coinciding with the 135th anniversary on July 18, 1998, of the 54th Massachusetts' valiant assault on Fort Wagner at the mouth of Charleston harbor, America dedicated a monument to the black soldiers and sailors and their white officers who fought for the North. The African American Civil War Memorial includes a nine-foot-tall bronze statue, *The Spirit of Freedom,* that honors both the veterans and the families they left behind to join the Federal Army and Navy. Another feature of the monument is a semicircular wall bearing the names of the nearly 209,000 black volunteers and their white commanders who, by example and deed, helped "form a more perfect Union." Maintained by the National Park Service, the attraction is located in the Shaw neighborhood—a Washington, D.C., community named for Robert Gould Shaw, the young colonel from Boston who died leading the heroic charge up the face of Fort Wagner. Schedule a trip to the memorial for what is a very moving and compelling connection to a forgotten part of our collective past. The National Park Service's home page contains information about the monument and how to reach it by way of the area's wonderful subway system.

"We Can, We Will"

Thousands of African American fighting men have proudly called themselves Buffalo Soldiers since the original all-black units were organized following the Civil War. One member of Troop M, 9th U.S. Cavalry, was Charles Davis, shown on the opposite page in an artistic rendering titled *Standing Tall.* Serving with distinction, the Virginia native received several commendations and was promoted to first sergeant. As it was, few blacks ever achieved officer status, even within their own segregated units. Many white commanders assigned to the all-black regiments did so under protest and considered the appointment a career killer. Only the third African American to graduate from West Point, Charles Young, who began his three decades in the Army with the fabled 9th Cavalry, became a notable exception to the institutional practice of summarily excluding blacks as officer candidates. Young's position as a commissioned officer did little to mitigate the stinging and repeated acts of racism directed at him by the civilian and military establishments. Rather than force his resignation, the abuse only strengthened Young's resolve to remain in the service. So successful was this son of former slaves in dealing with these challenges that he compiled an outstanding record, including a tour in the Philippines suppressing guerrilla groups. Prevailing political attitudes kept Young out of World War I, despite his repeated requests to be sent overseas with a combat unit. He died in 1922, a victim of kidney disease. Over 100,000 mourners lined the funeral route as Col. Charles Young was carried to his final resting place in Arlington National Cemetery.

The photographs featured on pages 40 and 41 were reproduced from the only copy known to still exist of a yearbook published about and for troopers serving with the 9th U.S. Cavalry. A prized possession of Sergeant Davis's great-great-nephew, Edwin J. Ford, Jr., of Winchester, Virginia, the book depicts some of what the men experienced as they worked to uphold the meaning of the regiment's motto, "We can, we will." All of these illustrations, including *Standing Tall,* are presented here with gratitude to Mr. Ford for his kind assistance.

First Sgt. Charles Davis of White Post, Virginia, is depicted in the watercolor *Standing Tall.* Like Colonel Young, Sergeant Davis is buried in Arlington National Cemetery.

Troop M, 9th U.S. Cavalry. Holding the unit's guidon at the end of the first row is Sergeant Davis.

The 9th Cavalry's machine gun platoon poses for its yearbook photo.

Field staff—commissioned officers, 9th Cavalry. Charles Young is seated fifth from the left in the first row.

The 9th Cavalry athletic team practices a mounted drill.

The Alert by Frederic Remington. During his years in the American outback, Remington provided future generations with a remarkable record of frontier life. Much of this time was spent traveling between the different military posts dotting the region, frequently riding with the cavalry regiments stationed across the seemingly endless stretches of Western wilderness. He was especially intrigued by the all-black units and found them to comprise some of the most dedicated soldiers in the Army. After accompanying a scouting party from the 10th Cavalry, Remington wrote, "They may be tired and they may be hungry, but they do not see fit to augment their misery by finding fault with everybody and everything. In this particular they are charming men with whom to serve . . . . As to their bravery: 'Will they fight?' That is easily answered. They have fought many, many times." Painted in 1888, *The Alert* is just one of Remington's many artistic creations that illustrates something of the pride and professionalism characterizing the African American horse soldiers of the Old West. *Courtesy Frederic Remington Art Museum, Ogdensburg, New York, with special thanks to Amy Furgison.*

CHAPTER FOUR

Medals for the Milkmaid

IN addition to managing the permanent collection housed in the newer part of the CIA Headquarters building, I also designed a number of thematic displays, usually to commemorate some notable—and perhaps overlooked—person or event. These ran for a specific length of time and included privately held memorabilia and graphics expressly loaned for the project, often by family members of the individuals highlighted in the presentation. With their appearance in the Exhibit Center-sponsored display, many of these artifacts were viewed publicly for the first time; some were even featured in newspaper articles and television programs that resulted when reporters were granted limited access to the building exclusively for this purpose.

To help the Agency celebrate its 50th birthday in 1997, I created a display that focused on several Office of Strategic Services (OSS) and early CIA veterans. Throughout the months preceding the production's June unveiling, a variety of packages arrived at my office, their valuable contents destined for the new cases set aside for the golden anniversary exhibit. One carton in particular was so heavy three people were required to safely handle it. Still another bearing the same return address in nearby Maryland was no larger than a shoe box and fit comfortably on the shelf where I stored historical curios borrowed for coming attractions.

While carefully dissecting these two parcels, my staff and I discovered several items that once belonged to a female operative whose lifetime of achievement is just now being recognized. From the smaller container we removed an authentic Distinguished Service Cross and a rare Member of the British

Empire medal. Packed around these were a dozen or so passports, their numerous and assorted country stamps suggesting something about the career and travels of the American agent to whom they were issued. In the unwieldy carton was the actual field radio she used while surreptitiously working behind the lines in occupied France during the Second World War. Finally, I thought to myself, I can ***really*** tell the story of Virginia Hall.

Until the arrival of this treasured memorabilia, only a poster-size photograph hanging in the Exhibit Center above OSS director William Donovan's desk suggested anything of Virginia's significant contributions to American espionage. As groups passed through the Center, I usually asked them to take note of the handsome wooden furnishing and compare it to the one visible in the picture featuring Virginia Hall. It was the same object, and Virginia was depicted leaning over the desk examining the Distinguished Service Cross the general had just presented to her at OSS Headquarters in downtown Washington. This was one of the two medals we had delicately unwrapped on a white sheet covering the worktable in our office. Along with the other artifacts, the awards had been sent by Virginia's niece, Lorna Catling, who was graciously sharing the items for the special 50th anniversary exhibit. I was hopeful these extraordinary pieces would allow me to better illustrate and convey something of the American woman the Gestapo considered "one of the most dangerous Allied agents in France."

Introducing my talks on Virginia, I knew few of those listening, including a large percentage of CIA employees, would have any idea of who she was. Once, when she was the subject of a "Name That HUMINT" question, a young man identified Virginia Hall as a dorm at the University of Virginia. Close, but no caltrop. My Virginia Hall was a World War II spy whose courage, devotion, and ingenuity earned her the two decorations shipped to me in early 1997.

Together with the radio and passports, it was particularly fitting that these prestigious awards were displayed at the Agency as part of its birthday gala: following her undercover work for the OSS in World War II, Virginia became one of the CIA's first female operatives after the post-war intelligence organization was established in 1947.

That Virginia's legacy was largely lost until only recently is not surprising. In many respects, that is the hallmark of a good and conscientious intelligence professional. These dedicated men and women do their duty quietly, many times putting themselves in great peril while carrying out their assigned missions. Living in the shadows, they shun the limelight even after many years into retirement. So it was with Virginia. Half a century later, however, her story is surfacing from declassified government records and from the personal recollections of her former colleagues, both male and female, who still marvel at the accomplishments of the "Limping Lady of the OSS."

Yes, limping. Virginia lost her left leg below the knee to a hunting accident long before joining the British intelligence service, the Special Operations Executive (SOE), in March 1941 and William Donovan's OSS three years later. To help conceal the fact she wore a wooden leg, Virginia learned to walk with a swinging motion, forsaking the aristocratic bearing by which she had been identified and recognized. Throughout a 25-year intelligence career, the determined and resourceful operative expected and received no special favors or allowances because of the artificial limb.

This is but one facet of Virginia's incredible life that, when told to groups of visitors in the Exhibit Center, moved most to ask for more information about her. I was delighted to oblige.

Virginia Hall was born to an upper-class Baltimore family on April 6, 1906. Gifted with a wide range of interests and abilities, she excelled in both academics and sports. Summers were happily spent on the family farm where Dindy, as she was known to relatives and close friends, enjoyed helping with the daily routine of chores. Later, when she was assigned to occupied France with the OSS, Virginia's experience milking cows and goats while growing up allowed the agent to establish and live her cover as a French milkmaid. Also useful was her extensive study of German, Italian, French, and Russian; at various times, Virginia had attended Radcliffe College, Barnard College, and The George Washington University here in the states, as well as several European universities. No matter where the elegant woman with the charming smile might be posted during her desired foreign service career, she would likely have a good working knowledge of the language spoken by the locals. Despite several overseas tours with the State Department as a clerk, however, Virginia was denied entrance into its professional ranks. This was a time when females in general and particularly those with a "disability" were relegated to lower-paying jobs that promised little chance for advancement.

Not content to simply ride out her career behind a desk, Virginia resigned from the State Department and began traveling across Europe. Once World War II erupted, she wasted little time volunteering for duty. Initially, Virginia drove medical transports for the French Ambulance Service. Later she was employed as a code clerk and then as an accountant for the U.S. military attaché in London. After only six months at the Embassy, the 35-year-old American was selected for operational work by the SOE. The British wartime intelligence organization drilled the Yankee woman with the wooden prosthesis in the finer points of weaponry, communications, and security measures. She took this training back into France as the SOE's first female field officer, establishing productive and respected agent networks while working undercover as a journalist.

With her colleagues in the resistance movement, Virginia helped smuggle downed Allied pilots and escaped prisoners of war out of the country. She also secured weapons and safe houses for use by French nationals secretly fighting the Germans. For her outstanding service while assigned to the SOE, Virginia Hall was awarded the Member of the British Empire medal in the name of King George VI.

Virginia continued her impressive World War II service with America's OSS. She wanted her salary deposited in her mother's bank account in Maryland, something difficult to do as a British agent. There was also the very practical consideration of death benefits. Working for the OSS, Virginia was supposed to be insured for $10,000, with her mother named as beneficiary. (Government paperwork being what it is, the proper forms were never processed.)

So, for a monthly salary of $336, Virginia signed on with William Donovan's intelligence agency and returned to France. Because her identity and reputation were well known to German authorities, she faced grave and constant danger.

But the Limping Lady's familiarity with the countryside, along with her considerable language expertise, served her well. In addition, she had acquired two very critical skills before joining the American intelligence effort: the knowledge of Morse code and the ability to operate a wireless radio.

Coming ashore on the Brittany coast, Virginia began her OSS service as plans were being finalized for history's largest amphibious landing just to the north at Normandy. Code-named "Diane," she set about creating an underground web of supporters, spies, and saboteurs using many of the contacts she had made during her years with the SOE. To maintain her cover of a milkmaid, Virginia labored on local farms. Dressed as a peasant, the woman once described in her college yearbook as "different and capricious" tended to the livestock and vegetable gardens. While herding cattle, she took note of especially flat and open fields that could serve as drop zones for Allied paratroopers. Milk deliveries to towns overrun with German soldiers were many times prearranged covert meetings with her connections in the French resistance.

Despite these full and often harrowing days, Virginia did not neglect the wireless. Disappearing into an elevated location (to enhance the signal), she quietly used the radio. Carefully "Diane" tapped out messages in Morse code concerning, among other subjects, the disposition of enemy troops in the area. She then waited for a response from headquarters. With their replies, officials in London might include orders for another assignment or news of double agents fingered by trustworthy sources. The radio we pulled from the heavily taped box 53 summers later was the same one Virginia had used in remote attics and haylofts in occupied France.

Virginia's work took on an even greater importance and urgency once D-Day unfolded on June 6, 1944. As the Allies pushed through Hitler's Atlantic Wall and across the beachheads, three battalions of French commandos—supervised, trained, and armed by the Limping Lady—engaged the Germans in guerrilla warfare, slowing their ability to react quickly and effectively to the advancing armies. During one mission, several of her partisans ambushed a Nazi convoy, taking 500 prisoners and inflicting 150 casualties.

For her gallantry and courage, Virginia was named a

recipient of the Distinguished Service Cross, making her the first civilian female so honored. Officials decided President Truman would personally confer the decoration, second only to the Medal of Honor, on the dauntless operative. However, when the cable arrived informing Virginia of these plans, she thought about the publicity a White House ceremony would generate, and how such attention might jeopardize her current and future undercover operations. She wired back from a liberated Paris: "No, I still have work to do here."

On September 27, 1945, General Donovan awarded the medal to the remarkable field agent at his E Street office with only her mother in attendance. This presentation was the subject of the photograph of Virginia I had always pointed out to visitors when discussing Donovan and his desk. A little over five decades after she received the Distinguished Service Cross at OSS Headquarters, it was on display at CIA Headquarters, along with other personal effects representing the career of the trailblazing woman who so nobly and ably served the cause of freedom in both war and peace.

Virginia Hall died in 1982. Those of us intrigued by her life and enriched by her example are left to wonder how she would view all the attention suddenly directed toward her. We hope Dindy would forgive our intrusion into her private and professional personas. For she is, as one of her admiring associates wrote after the war, "an inspiration to all."

Throughout history, women have contributed to espionage activities in a variety of ways, many times at great personal risk and sacrifice. In World War II alone, nearly 4,000 women proudly served in William Donovan's OSS. Some were employed as couriers, cartographers, or clerks; others, like Virginia Hall, repeatedly and unselfishly put themselves in harm's way as field agents working behind enemy lines. Yet another was Elizabeth (Betty) McIntosh, a veteran of both the OSS and the CIA. In May 1998, Betty's revealing book detailing the exploits of these unheralded patriots (some of whom she knew personally) was released. Titled *Sisterhood of Spies: The Women of the OSS,* the 282-page hardback includes an entire chapter devoted to Virginia Hall. Closing out her section on Dindy, Betty paid tribute to this exemplary American, calling her "a legend to many of the OSS women . . .[T]o this day she is revered as one of the true heroines of the war." Young women especially will find this book engrossing and its message immensely appealing and rewarding. It is published by the Naval Institute Press in Annapolis, Maryland, and copies should be available in larger retail outlets; in addition, the book can most probably be purchased via the Internet from one of several online distributors. If you have problems locating it, contact the publisher at 1 (800) 233-8764 or look for the Naval Institute Press Web site on the Internet.

Virginia Hall receives the Distinguished Service Cross from General Donovan on September 27, 1945. *Courtesy Lorna Catling, Baltimore, Maryland. Ms. Catling is Virginia Hall's niece.*

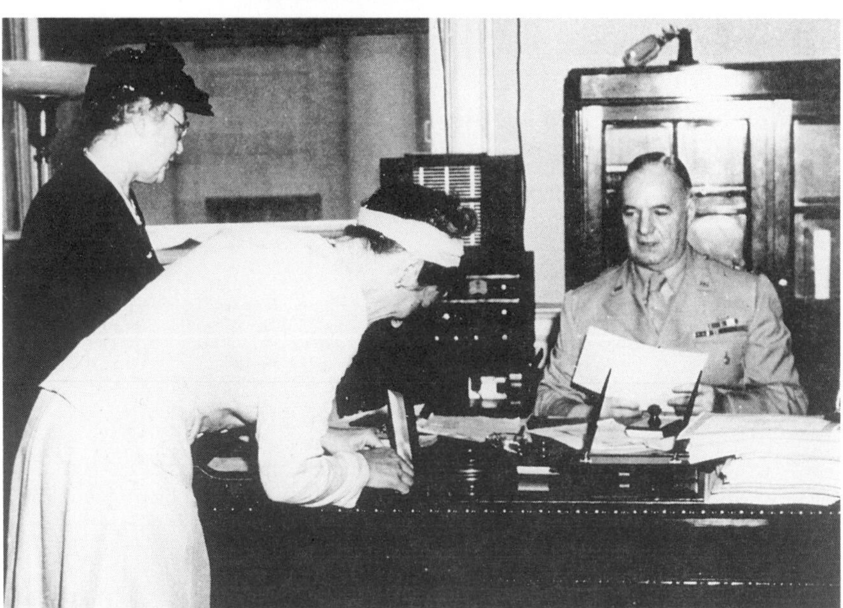

Reproduction of the photo that hung in the CIA Exhibit Center of Virginia Hall examining her Distinguished Service Cross in Donovan's office. Looking on is Virginia's mother. The general's desk became part of the Exhibit Center's permanent collection in 1994. *Courtesy Lorna Catling.*

Dindy and friends. The OSS operative's childhood experiences working on the family farm helped Virginia maintain her milkmaid cover when she was stationed behind the lines in France. *Courtesy Lorna Catling.*

Distinguished Service Cross (left) and Member of the British Empire awarded to Virginia Hall. As part of the CIA's 50th anniversary commemoration, these medals were displayed at the Agency, marking their first-ever public exhibition. *Courtesy CIA Exhibit Center.*

Agency employee Jeanne Vertefeuille in the CIA Exhibit Center with Virginia Hall's field radio while it was on loan to the Center. Vertefeuille's uncompromising and exhaustive investigation of CIA mole Aldrich Ames led to his guilty plea in 1994 on charges of spying for the former Soviet Union. *Courtesy Elizabeth McIntosh and Bernard Van Leer.*

CHAPTER FIVE

The Uncrackable Code

SITUATED securely on the bottom of the case in the Exhibit Center containing World War II-era memorabilia was an actual Enigma machine—one of Germany's fabled encrypting devices that produced different ciphers to protect communications. A system whereby each letter or number in a message is replaced with another letter or number, ciphers in some form have been utilized by individuals, armies, and governments down through history (remember the brass cipher disks of the Civil War?). As technology has advanced, so, too, has the ability to encipher mechanically delivered transmissions. The battery-powered Enigma machines of the 20th century were engineering wonders whose intricate network of plugs and wiring belied their portability and operational simplicity. A combat veteran of the Second World War, the Enigma machine displayed in the Center was fully functional, thanks to some minor repairs made with materials obtained from a local Radio Shack.

Originally manufactured to pass and receive business messages, various types of Enigma were utilized by Hitler's Germany to encipher and decipher military and diplomatic communications. It took considerable time and talent, but Allied cryptographers ultimately forced Enigma to surrender its secrets. Relying on several versions of their own electromechanical wizard called the Bombe, these dedicated (if overworked) men and women were finally able to figure out most of the settings used to disguise Enigma messages; on a three-rotor model like the one featured in the Center, the possible encrypting patterns totaled over one trillion.

Spearheading the intensive effort to neutralize Enigma were British cryptographers and their colleagues operating out of an imposing Victorian mansion known as Bletchley Park. Located about 40 miles north of London, the secret government facility with its hastily constructed wooden barracks had housed a total of nearly 12,000 workers over the course of the war. Many of these were Americans. Bletchley Park is now managed as a publicly accessible museum, where a growing collection of the technological triumphs that compromised German communications is being preserved and restored.

The campaign to crack Enigma-generated encryptions was helped along in no small measure by the Third Reich's overreliance on the celebrated devices. Incorrectly, as it turned out, Nazi cryptographic experts assumed their Allied counterparts would prove incapable of working through the massive mathematical calculations required to decipher Enigma transmissions. This costly error in judgment encouraged the Germans to use the system for messages that did not really need protection, creating even more pieces of the Enigma puzzle that could (and did) fall into British and American hands.

Providing the Allies with the technical means to break Germany's venerable communications encrypting system was not the Bombes' only contribution, however. Of equal importance was the role development of the electromagnetic monsters would play in the evolution of modern computers. Today's sophisticated personal computers are actually engineering descendants of the eight-foot-high super-calculators that made Enigma less of an enigma during World War II, facilitating such crucial battles as those waged against Hitler's deadly U-boats in the Atlantic.

Also displayed in the Center was a photograph illustrating the story of another method developed to send secret communications during World War II; unlike Enigma, this cleverly devised system, which was actually a code, survived the war intact.

Instead of substituting individual letters and numbers (as with Enigma and its ciphers), codes rely on complete words, phrases, symbols, or groupings of numbers to conceal the contents of a message. The ingenious code highlighted in the Exhibit Center wall hanging was based upon a little known and largely undocumented language from the American Southwest. Pictured were two U.S. Marines transmitting a voice message over a field radio using their remarkable encoding system. Not typical recruits, these young men were actually military cryptographers stationed in the Pacific Theater during the last three years of the war as part of the Navajo code talker program.

The approximately 300 Navajos who saw duty as code talkers disguised messages using expressions adapted from their own language that corresponded with the desired term. To describe amphibious actions, the Navajo word for "frog" was used. Sailors were "white hats." Observation planes were "owls"; grenades were "potatoes." The Navajo phrase for "our mother" was the code talkers' way of saying America. These and many other idioms evolved into an extremely complicated—and impenetrable—encrypting system.

Determined to protect the code and its origin at all costs, officials banned printed lists of the coined words and their meanings except in a very few instances. This required that each Navajo commit the entire code to memory. In addition, personal letters the men sent home were not delivered. While this practice kept the correspondence from falling into the hands of the Japanese and their confederates, it created a particular hardship for the families, who had no word concerning the welfare of a husband, father, son, brother, or uncle.

Until the initial wave of two-man code talker teams was ordered to Guadalcanal in 1942, the Japanese had repeatedly demonstrated a maddening ability to decode American military radio communications; impressive wiretapping skills allowed them to intercept the messages almost at will. Listening in on Marine voice transmissions sent by the code talkers, however, Japanese SIGINT snoopers heard nothing but incomprehensible and unrecognizable sounds. Most were accomplished English speakers who had attended some of America's best universities prior to the war. None of their studies, in Japan or in the United States, had in any way prepared them for what they were picking up on the wiretaps. Further frustrating enemy eavesdroppers was the fact that Navajo was essentially an unwritten language at the time of World War II; consequently, if Japanese cryptographers did somehow manage to trace the origin of the strange guttural tones characterizing the messages, there still was no formal compilation of the odd phrases and their definitions to use as a reference aid.

After the code talkers hit the beachheads of the Pacific, Marine radio communications sent across the region were effectively shielded, making a number of critical victories possible. Not the least of these was the battle for Iwo Jima during February and March 1945, one of the bloodiest contests of the entire war. During the first two days of fighting, code talkers worked nonstop, sending and receiving over 800 error-free messages. Many military historians believe the island would not have fallen to the advancing American units without the invaluable contributions of these brave and dedicated Marine cryptographers. At one point during the horrific battle, the Stars and Stripes was victoriously raised on Mount Suribachi, located at the southern tip of Iwo Jima. News of the epic moment was initially relayed by Navajos using the code that played such a crucial role in the struggle.

Captured on film for the world by Associated Press photographer Joe Rosenthal, the memorable photograph of five Marines and one Navy hospital corpsman pressing the banner and its makeshift flagpole upright earned Rosenthal a Pulitzer Prize. Following the war, this stirring event was immortalized in bronze by sculptor Felix de Weldon. His 78-foot-high statue now stands on a grassy knoll near Arlington National Cemetery as a memorial to all Marines killed in action since 1775.

Another ferocious engagement in which the code talkers distinguished themselves unfolded on Saipan, a strategically important site that the U.S. Army Air Forces hoped to use as a principal staging area for B-29 strikes against enemy strongholds. At one point in the fighting, code talkers transmitted a message halting hours of friendly fire that had threatened an entire American battalion trying to take the island.

While the Navajos garnered numerous medals and commendations for their valor and service, they paid a price: on Iwo Jima alone, three code talkers were killed during the month-long battle.

Despite the deadly realities of combat that constantly surrounded them, the cryptographers stayed true to the Marine Corps motto, *Semper Fidelis*—always faithful. Several felt the ability to remain focused as explosives and bullets ripped through the air stemmed from the traditional teachings of their childhood; in addition, many believed the Great Spirit was watching over them. Back home on the 27,000 square miles of Arizona, New Mexico, and Utah that comprise the Navajo Nation, family members conducted ancient ceremonial rites to help ensure the safety of a loved one, often using clothes the code talker had worn before joining the Marines.

Warfare, with all its inherent perils, was not the only challenge the Navajo code talkers faced. Since most had never been off tribal land before enlisting, some had to deal with a powerful culture shock that marked their first few weeks in boot camp. This was especially problematic for the youngest recruits. A few were only 15 when they were selected for the special cryptographic program, so great was the demand for an indecipherable code and for enough trained personnel who could quickly and accurately transmit and receive messages using it.

Arriving overseas, the Navajos were further tested by an assortment of unusual and trying circumstances. One notable difficulty arose from their unfamiliarity to most American fighting men. Because the majority of Army troops serving alongside the Marines had never seen a Navajo, there were times when a code talker was mistakenly captured by an unwitting GI who thought he had encountered a Japanese infiltrator. Reports the "enemy prisoner" was wearing a regulation Marine combat uniform and government-issued identification tags only complicated matters. Once the soldier learned he had actually snared a fellow American, there came the embarrassing revelation that this particular "POW" was a member of a highly prized group of U.S. military cryptographers. In an effort to curb the number of these potentially dangerous incidents, and as a measure of the value field commanders eventually placed on the encoding system and the men who made it work, the Marines assigned every code talker a personal bodyguard.

That the Navajos could contribute to the war effort in their own unique way was a source of quiet satisfaction to the code talkers. Asked about their service in the Pacific, most would later say they were Americans who simply did their duty. When the cryptographers' reputation began to spread from island to island, however, one bit of irony was never far from the minds of those who knew something of the Navajos and their heritage: the language so integral to the uncrackable code safeguarding Marine communications in the imperiled Pacific Theater was the same one Navajos had been discouraged, even forbidden, from speaking in many reservation schools. Still others questioned the fairness of continuing to limit the Navajos' right to vote as military officials combed the desolate and rugged roadways of the Southwest looking for able recruits.

After Japan and Germany surrendered, most code talkers returned to their tribal lands and families. Invoking traditional Navajo purification ceremonies, many of the veterans sought to spiritually cleanse themselves, washing away what they could of the traumatic memories that followed them home. As for the matter of expanded voting privileges, it took another 12 years before all eligible Navajos could fully exercise this basic right of citizenship.

It was not until 1968 that the Navajo code was declassified and the men could talk about it publicly if they wished. While mindful of the basic Navajo caveats prohibiting the glorification of warfare, many code talkers do share something of their amazing cryptographic achievements with educational and civic organizations. In November 1993, two of these inspirational patriots visited the CIA for its annual Native American Month celebration. As part of the presentation, the code talkers demonstrated their extraordinary system to the audience. Before a packed house that included then Director of Central Intelligence R. James Woolsey, the former Marines encoded, transmitted, and then decoded a specially selected message. It was the biblical verse carved on the south wall of the CIA Headquarters lobby: *"And ye shall know the truth and the truth shall make you free." — John VIII - XXXII*

It is not often you can meet an individual who made history over a half-century ago, but that is the case with many of the Navajo code talkers. A number belong to the Navajo Code Talkers Association and take great pleasure in recounting some of their adventures in person before school and community groups. Moreover, the association maintains a library of audio recordings featuring taped interviews with some of these heroic Marines. For further information, contact Albert Smith, a code talker veteran who serves as president of the group, at P.O. Box 416, Window Rock, Arizona 86515.

An increasing number of publicly accessible exhibits are popularizing the code talkers' story. One in particular is featured at the Pentagon. Dedicated in 1992 as part of the nationwide commemoration honoring the 50th anniversary of World War II, the permanent display is a regular stop on the Pentagon tour. Call the Defense Department at (703) 695-1776 or log onto its Web site for more details about visiting this historic Federal building across the Potomac River from Washington.

The Gallup-McKinley (New Mexico) Chamber of Commerce offers an exhibit on the code talkers that has attracted a good deal of interest. A variety of artifacts can be viewed, including some of the radios the men used in the Pacific. Call the Chamber at (505) 722-2228 for details.

If you would like to explore the larger topic of codes and codebreakers, the National Cryptologic Museum located near the National Security Agency at Fort Meade, Maryland, is a fantastic place for such an adventure. Visitors can experience for free a wide variety of exhibits that highlight the evolution and use of codes throughout history. Find out all this attraction has to offer by calling the museum at (301) 688-5849 or by logging onto its impressive Internet site.

The Web site maintained by the Bletchley Park Trust also deserves a close look. Click on this intriguing computer link to the British museum, which is working to protect and restore many of the original machines developed to crack Axis codes—devices that are the forerunners of the PC and laptop you are using to take your cybertour.

Finally, while you are in the Washington, D.C., area, be sure to see Felix de Weldon's magnificent and moving statue depicting the flag raising on Mount Suribachi. Throughout the summer, the Marines' renowned band and silent drill team stage a series of colorful and inspirational outdoor ceremonies at the site near Arlington National Cemetery, called the Marine Corps (or Iwo Jima) Memorial. They are free and open to the public. Contact the Marine Corps Public Events office at (703) 614-1034 for more information. Bring a blanket and enjoy the ride.

Three-rotor Enigma machine displayed in the CIA Exhibit Center. In an effort to thwart Allied cryptographers, the Germans frequently changed the rotor settings of each device. *Courtesy CIA Exhibit Center.*

Photograph of Navajo code talkers featured in the CIA Exhibit Center. Cpl. Henry Bake, Jr., (left) and Pfc. George Kirk of a Marine Signal Unit are pictured operating their radio on Bougainville, largest of the Solomon Islands. The code used by the Navajos during World War II was never broken by the enemy—a feat not accomplished during any previous war in recorded history. *Courtesy United States Marine Corps.*

United States Marine Corps Memorial, Arlington, Virginia. Often called the Iwo Jima Memorial, the statue is a popular tourist attraction. One of the six servicemen depicted planting the Stars and Stripes on Mount Suribachi is Ira Hayes, a Pima Indian from Arizona who served as a combat Marine. He was buried with honors in nearby Arlington National Cemetery after his body lay in state in the Arizona State Capitol. *Photograph by the author.*

CHAPTER SIX

Snagging Pop Flies and Spies

PERHAPS the most popular attraction in the CIA Exhibit Center for kids of all ages while I was curator were the cases housing memorabilia from the 15-year major league baseball career of Morris "Moe" Berg. Featured was the bat he used to hammer his sixth and final home run—a feat the 6'1", 185-pound righthander accomplished in 1939 during his last game as a professional player. Two of Moe's baseball cards were also on display. On the full-color card, Moe was shown behind the plate for the Washington Senators; the other depicted the catcher as a member of his fifth and last team, the Boston Red Sox. Of the remaining items, one in particular suggested something of the major leaguer's other life. It was a reproduction of a pass he was issued permitting him to attend sessions of the Nuremberg Trials where Nazis were prosecuted for wartime criminal acts. Moe's signature was clearly visible on the enlarged copy. (The original was always secured in a vault to protect it from light and loss.) Many professional athletes sign their respective sports cards; Moe's autograph can be found on ephemera more often associated with the front page of a newspaper than the sports page.

Moe Berg has been called baseball's Renaissance man because of his keen interest in and ability to comprehend so many diverse and intellectually challenging topics. Dubbed "Professor Berg" by a host of newspaper columnists and teammates, the popular player enjoyed studying and speaking foreign languages as much as he did snagging pop flies over home plate. Endowed with a natural curiosity for all things scientific, Moe was also able to teach himself enough about physics to understand how atoms can be split to create energy.

During World War II, the former ballplayer, whose friends included Babe Ruth, Will Rogers, and Albert Einstein, used all of these special talents as an overseas operative for the Office of Strategic Services.

On one mission in December 1944, officials sent Moe into Switzerland to hear a talk by Werner Heisenberg, Germany's premier nuclear physicist. Moe was to determine from Heisenberg's speech if Germany was producing something similar to what America was creating with its super-secret Manhattan Project—an atomic bomb. Since Heisenberg was the Third Reich's most esteemed scientist, he surely would be part of the historic undertaking. Moe was issued a pistol for this mission. If Heisenberg's lecture suggested Germany was building its own version of the most powerful weapon ever conceived, the undercover OSS agent had orders to shoot him on the spot. Removing the Nobel Prize winner and his considerable intellect from the equation, the thinking was, would effectively slow Hitler's atomic program, giving the advantage to the Americans. Moe did not draw the gun: nothing in Heisenberg's speech hinted such an effort existed.

Later that week, at a small party hosted for the scientist which Moe attended, Heisenberg essentially said as much. During the get-together, Heisenberg acknowledged that Germany, in reality, had already been defeated—a particularly intriguing admission since it would be another five months before Hitler's forces actually surrendered. If the Nazis had anything on the order of the Manhattan Project under development, Heisenberg's feelings concerning his country's immediate future probably would have been considerably more upbeat. When filing his report, Moe took special note of the physicist's revealing, if somewhat despondent, concession.

At long last, American leaders had something of the assurance they were seeking that Germany was not producing an atomic bomb.

There was another aspect to the former big leaguer's work during this time that proved of great value. Because Moe and other field operatives had learned the location of many of Hitler's most celebrated academicians, American and British personnel were able to remove a number of them, including Heisenberg, to England from Germany. This kept the intellectuals—and their wealth of scientific expertise—from falling into the hands of Josef Stalin's advancing Red Army.

Moe also served in war-ravaged Italy. For one especially critical assignment, he established a friendship with aeronautical engineer Antonio Ferri, whose discoveries surrounding the principles of supersonic flight were of immense interest to the National Advisory Committee on Aeronautics, forerunner of NASA. After several meetings, including some spent teaching the Ferri children baseball, Moe persuaded the scientist to come to America. When hearing of Moe's role in successfully encouraging Ferri and his family to leave their homeland for the United States, President Franklin Roosevelt is said to have remarked, "I see Berg is still catching pretty well."

That this son of Ukrainian immigrants could lead the different lives he did—as a nationally known ballplayer with a gift of genius and later as a successful wartime secret operative—says as much about his inherent intellect as it does about his complex personality. In 1923, Moe graduated magna cum laude from Princeton with a degree in modern languages. After a three-month stint with the Brooklyn Robins (soon to be Dodgers), he enrolled in the famed Sorbonne in Paris, where his French-speaking ability so impressed administrators that they waived his tuition charges. For a year he happily studied experimental phonetics under some of the greatest linguists in Europe. Returning to the United States, Moe attended Columbia University's School of Law. Using money he made playing for the Chicago White Sox, the batterymate of future Hall of Famer Ted Lyons earned a law degree during the off-season and was later admitted to the New York Bar.

Moe's love of languages—some say he spoke eight, others say it was closer to a dozen—served him well not only in the world of spying, but also on the ball field. While at Princeton, Moe played shortstop. He and the Tigers' second baseman devised a method of signaling each other during a game using words in Latin. Unless an opposing player was familiar with the ancient language, he would have little idea what Moe and his teammate were up to. While playing with the 1933 pennant-winning Senators, Moe kept a tuxedo in his locker at Griffith Stadium for those evenings when he attended a formal gathering at one of the many embassies located in the nation's capital. Because the catcher more often than not had a working knowledge of the host country's native tongue, he was a regular at these affairs.

Languages also helped Moe become a national media personality. His appearance on the popular radio program *Information, Please!* (similar to today's television program *Jeopardy*) resulted in hundreds of fan letters from listeners. The major leaguer's considerable knowledge about the game of baseball and those who played it had little to do with his success on the radio show; rather, he did well because he could easily answer such esoteric questions as the origin of the name Dorothy. (As Moe correctly responded, the name is derived from the Greek word for "gift of God.")

For all this lore, Moe is often relegated to footnotes in the many books written about baseball and its heroes. Besides Lyons and Ruth, some of his colleagues included Boston greats Jimmie Foxx and Ted Williams. Moe's .243 lifetime batting average wasn't all that impressive compared to these legends. But it was his tremendous baseball savvy and slingshot arm that kept him in the game more than a decade after he suffered a knee injury in 1930 while playing for the White Sox.

Moe Berg loved everything about baseball, especially its mental aspects. But Moe's father often bemoaned his youngest son's choice of vocations, preferring instead he abandon baseball for the legal profession. Coming to his sibling's defense at one point was Moe's brother, himself a medical doctor. During the horrible period of the Great Depression, Dr. Sam reminded the senior Berg that Moe was able to earn a respectable living at a time when many of his former Princeton classmates could not.

The Exhibit Center display about Moe only slightly suggested something of this accomplished and patriotic American. He really did not have to forsake his comfortable life in the majors, with all its attendant benefits. Before finishing out his baseball career as a coach with Boston in 1942, however, Moe took stock of the disintegrating situation unfolding beyond the ballpark and across the Atlantic. "Europe is in flames, withering in a fire set by Hitler," he told a New York sportswriter. "All over that continent, men and women and children are dying. Soon we, too, will be involved. And what am I doing? I'm sitting in the bullpen, telling jokes to the relief pitchers." So it was that this intellectually gifted catcher, who is considered one of the first big league Jewish players of note, wound up overseas fighting the evils of the Third Reich as an operative for William Donovan's OSS.

On May 29, 1972, Moe Berg's extraordinary life came to an end at the age of 70. Ever the baseball buff, he spoke his last words to one of the hospital nurses caring for him: "How are the Mets doing today?"

For titles about Moe Berg or on the larger topic of sports figures who served their country during wartime, spend an afternoon at your local library exploring the numerous entries included on the different data bases. (Many players, like Hall of Famer Ted Williams, came home decorated military heroes.)

Some of Moe's personal papers are archived in the New York Public Library. Included in these holdings is correspondence he maintained with everyone from scientists to sports greats. For further details about accessing the documents, donated by the ballplayer's family following his death, call the helpful staff in the Manuscripts and Archives Division at (212) 930-0801.

The National Baseball Hall of Fame and Museum in Cooperstown, New York, has some of Moe's artifacts including the Medal of Freedom he was awarded for his espionage work with the OSS. For information about hours and admission charges, telephone the museum at 1 (888) 425-5633 or visit its home page on the Internet.

Ted Williams, Moe's onetime Red Sox teammate, has established his own Museum and Hitters Hall of Fame in Hernando, Florida. Much of the "Splendid Splinter's" memorabilia, including items representing his military service in the Second World War and Korea, are displayed here. Call the good people at the museum—(352) 527-6566—for more information or check the museum's Web site on the Internet.

Morris "Moe" Berg at the centennial of baseball game in 1939. During his 15-year baseball career, Moe played for five major professional teams: Brooklyn of the National League and Chicago, Cleveland, Washington, and Boston of the American League. *Courtesy Elizabeth Shames, Portland, Maine. Ms. Shames is Moe Berg's cousin.*

THE WASHINGTON CLUB, PENNANT WINNERS IN THE AMERICAN LEAGUE: In the front row, left to right—Rice, Stewart, Goslin, Schacht, Griffith, Mahoney, mascot (sitting), Cronin, Harris, Bolton and Altrock. Middle row, left to right—Russell, Thomas, Chapman, Travis, Burke, Kerr, Weaver, Myer. Back row, left to right—Sewell, Berg, Whitehill, Prim, Schulte, Manush, McColl, Bluege, Kuhel, Crowder and Boken.

American League champion Washington Senators, 1933. Moe Berg is pictured second from the left in the back row. (In what proved to be their last trip to the World Series, the Senators were defeated by the New York Giants four games to one.) *Author's collection.*

SA-1 (revised 11-1-

APPLICATION FOR EMPLOYMENT AND PERSONAL HISTORY STATEMENT

Instructions: 1. Answer all questions *completely*. If question does not apply write "not plicable." Write "unknown" only if you do not know the answer and cannot tain the answer from personal records. Use a separate sheet for extra det on any question or questions for which you do not have sufficient room.

2. Attach 2 recent passport size pictures to this form, date taken writte the back of each.

3. Type, print or write carefully; illegible or incomplete forms will not rece consideration.

HAVE YOU READ AND UNDERSTOOD THE INSTRUCTIONS? YES (Yes or No)

SEC. 1. PERSONAL BACKGROUND

A. FULL NAME Miss Mr. Mrs. MORRIS BERG TELEPHONE DISTRICT

PRESENT ADDRESS MAYFLOWER HOTEL WASHINGTON D.C. (St. & No. / City / State / Country)

LEGAL RESIDENCE 156 ROSEVILLE AVENUE NEWARK, NEW JERS (St. & No. / City / State / Country)

B. NICKNAME "MOE" ANY OTHER NAMES THAT YOU HAVE USED —

UNDER WHAT CIRCUMSTANCES HAVE YOU EVER USED THES NAMES? —

HOW LONG? — IF A LEGAL CHANGE, GIVE PARTICULARS — (When) — (Where) (By what authority?)

C. DATE OF BIRTH MARCH 2, 1902 PLACE OF BIRTH NEW YORK N.Y. U.S.A. (City / State / Country)

RACIAL ORIGIN THROUGH MOTHER JEWISH THROUGH FATHER JEWISH

D. PRESENT NATIONALITY AMERICAN BY BIRTH? YES BY MARRIAGE? —

BY NATURALIZATION CERTIFICATE # — ISSUED — (Date) BY — (Court)

AT — (City) — (State) — (Country)

HAVE YOU HAD A PREVIOUS NATIONALITY? NO WHAT? —

(663) HELD BETWEEN WHAT DATES? [illegible] ANY OTHER NATIONALITY? —

Moe Berg's application to join the OSS. Note the list of employers and job descriptions he has provided on the second page. *Courtesy CIA Exhibit Center.*

SEC. 20. FINANCIAL BACKGROUND (CONT'D)

GIVE three CREDIT REFERENCES – IN THE U.S.

NAME: NATIONAL NEWARK & ESSEX BANKING CO. ADDRESS BROAD STREET NEWARK, N.J. (St. & No. / City / State)

NAME: — ADDRESS (St. & No. / City / State)

NAME: ADDRESS (St. & No. / City / State)

SEC. 21. CHRONOLOGICAL HISTORY OF EMPLOYMENT FOR PAST 10 YEARS. INCLUDE CASUAL EMPLOYMENT. INCLUDE ALSO PERIODS OF UNEMPLOYMENT. GIVE ADDRESS AND STATE WHAT YOU DID DURING PERIODS OF UNEMPLOYMENT. INCLUDE LAST 5 POSITIONS AND COVER AT LEAST 10 YEARS.

EMPLOYER WASHINGTON BASEBALL CLUB TITLE OF JOB CATCHER

ADDRESS GRIFFITH STADIUM WASHINGTON, D.C. (St. & No. / City / State / Country)

YOUR DUTIES AND SPECIALTY CATCHER

KIND OF BUSINESS: BASEBALL NAME OF SUPERVISOR CLARK GRIFFITH

FROM: 1932 TO: 1934 SALARY $ PER

REASONS FOR LEAVING

EMPLOYER BOSTON AMERICAN B.B.C. TITLE OF JOB CATCHER AND COACH

ADDRESS FENWAY PARK BOSTON, MASSACHUSETTS (St. & No. / City / State / Country)

YOUR DUTIES AND SPECIALTY CATCHER AND COACH

KIND OF BUSINESS: BASEBALL NAME OF SUPERVISOR THOMAS A. YAWKEY

FROM: 1935 TO: 1941 SALARY $ PER

REASON FOR LEAVING TO BE CONSULTANT TO COORDINATOR INTERAM AFF.

EMPLOYER COORDINATOR INTERAMERICAN AFFAIRS TITLE OF JOB CHIEF CONSULTANT

ADDRESS COMMERCE DEPARTMENT BUILDING WASHINGTON, D.C. (St. & No. / City / State / Country)

YOUR DUTIES AND SPECIALTY CONSULTANT – CONFIDENTIAL – ARMED FORCE

KIND OF BUSINESS: WAR OFFICE NAME OF SUPERVISOR NELSON A. ROCKEFELL

FROM: 1942 TO: 1943 SALARY $ PER

REASONS FOR LEAVING RESIGNATION TO ACCEPT POSITION WITH O.S.S.

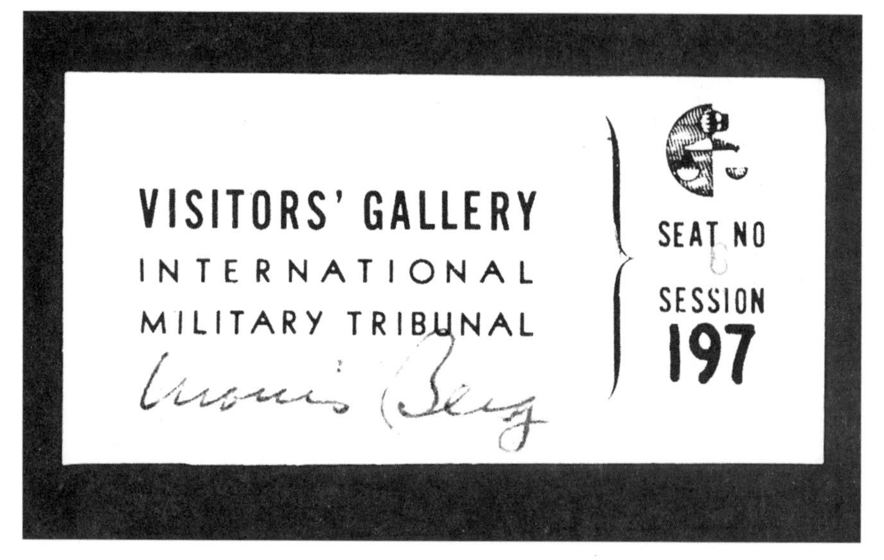

Pass to the Nuremberg Trials issued to Moe Berg. To gain admission to the proceedings that targeted Nazi war criminals, one of the major leagues' first Jewish ballplayers had to personally sign his pass. *Author's collection.*

CHAPTER SEVEN

Name That HUMINT

HERE are some of the more popular "Name That HUMINT" questions that challenged visitors to the CIA Exhibit Center while I was curator. The answers are also included, proving this is not the kind of test that can cost a contestant a National Merit Scholarship if incorrect responses outnumber correct ones. (Don't feel badly if that happens; many career CIA employees didn't get the right answers either.) HAVE FUN.

1. Who is considered the first Director of Central Intelligence (DCI), the official responsible for overseeing all of the nation's various intelligence organizations, including the CIA?

A. George Washington. While there was nothing like the OSS or the CIA in place during the American Revolution, Washington, as a military strategist and commander in chief of the Continental Army, knew the value of good intelligence and the field operatives supplying it, many of whom he paid out of his own pocket. The general's effective use of this information helped him defeat the numerically superior British forces who were better equipped and—for a time—better trained than the Colonials. DCI William Casey, named the country's top spy by President Ronald Reagan, once stated that "my first predecessor as Director of Central Intelligence was . . . George Washington, who appointed himself."

2. What is cryptography?

A. Literally, the word means "secret writing." In practice, cryptography is the science of passing messages in code or cipher. (Moe Berg would have known the answer to this one.) Cryptography in some form has been around for centuries. A sculpture by James Sanborn called *Kryptos* stands in one of the courtyards at CIA Headquarters. It is said a secret message (or two? or three?) is contained in the 2,000 letters that make up the artwork's encrypted copper screen.

3. Who is the "Father of American Cryptography?"

A. Thomas Jefferson, who developed a cipher system that was used to protect written communications concerning, among other topics, the drafting of the U.S. Constitution in 1787. Jefferson was serving as Minister to France while the rest of the Founding Fathers were working behind closed doors in sweltering Philadelphia creating a governmental framework for their new nation. To keep Jefferson apprised of developments concerning the convention, the unofficial recording secretary of the secret proceedings, James Madison, wrote the young emissary several letters outlining the work and direction of the 55 delegates. Correspondence sent through the mail system was susceptible to snooping, especially if it was pouched aboard ships for the very long voyage to Europe; consequently, Madison routinely encrypted dispatches he sent overseas to Jefferson. Using the system he had created and then shared with Madison, the diplomat deciphered the messages. In one particularly important communication, Jefferson learned from his friend that the delegates had decided upon a federal government made up of three branches.

One of America's foremost gadget gurus, the genius from Monticello later invented a six-inch-long, hand-held wooden apparatus he called a "wheel cypher." Cylindrical in shape, the device employed Jefferson's own method of encrypting and decrypting messages. Nearly two centuries after he created it, elements of the U.S. government and military were still using the third President's venerable system in their various wheel ciphers.

Thomas Jefferson by Rembrandt Peale. One of two life portraits that Peale painted of the master cryptographer, this oil hangs in the White House. It was in the Executive Mansion where Jefferson and Meriwether Lewis began planning in 1802 a then-secret expedition to explore lands west of the Mississippi, including those that the United States would fortuitously buy from Napoleon one year later as part of the Louisiana Purchase. Like most who have succeeded him in office, the nation's third chief executive understood the value of accurate information in conducting the affairs of state. As such, Lewis and Clark's two-year journey was actually an intelligence-gathering mission carried out by order of the President of the United States. In addition to locating and charting a Northwest Passage to the Pacific, the Corps of Discovery was tasked with obtaining as much data as possible about the region. Jefferson was especially interested in learning all he could about the different native inhabitants populating the expanse, as well as the varieties of wildlife and vegetation that flourished throughout it. For a better understanding of what his historic and unprecedented land acquisition actually encompassed, Jefferson relied on what is known today as HUMINT. *White House Collection. Courtesy of and copyrighted by the White House Historical Association, with special thanks to Harmony Haskins.*

4. This female scout and guide participated in an early 19th-century American intelligence-gathering mission, yet it is estimated that she was only 15 years old when she joined the all-male operation. Who was this woman and what was her role in an undertaking that has been compared to the modern-day exploration of space both in terms of its inherent danger and its importance to the nation? (Hint: this has to do with Mr. Jefferson and his real estate deal.)

A. Sacagawea, the Shoshone woman whose contributions to Lewis and Clark's epic expedition to the Pacific Ocean were instrumental in its successful outcome. When the Corps of Discovery needed horses, she arranged for several to be procured from a band of Shoshones led by her brother. Her work as an interpreter for the white men allowed them to carry out Jefferson's instructions that they establish peaceful contact with the indigenous peoples. Familiar with the various kinds of edible plants that grew throughout the region, she introduced the explorers to these fruits and vegetables, providing them with new food sources that not only helped sustain the travelers when supplies ran low but also added some important yet missing vitamins to their diet. Once, when a boat capsized, Sacagawea rescued most of its contents, including many of the notes and illustrations that chronicled the journey for Jefferson and future generations. After the expedition returned home, William Clark acknowledged Sacagawea's critical part in the two-year fact-finding trip: "[She] diserved [sic] a greater reward for her attention and services on that rout [sic] than we had in our power to give her."

Nearly two centuries after Sacagawea rendered her invaluable assistance to the Corps and its reconnaissance mission, the U.S. Mint plans to issue a new dollar coin featuring an image representing her. Scheduled for release in the year 2000, the coin will be in circulation in time for the start of the national bicentennial commemoration honoring the Lewis and Clark expedition three years later.

To gain a greater appreciation of Lewis and Clark and their place in our country's history, locate a copy of Stephen E. Ambrose's compelling and captivating work *Undaunted Courage: Meriwether Lewis, Thomas Jefferson, and the Opening of the American West.* The 511-page book gives the reader a sense that he or she is actually part of the perilous quest without having to leave the security and comfort of home. Published in 1996, it should still be available at most bookstores.

Many of the breathtaking natural wonders that the pioneering party confronted as they made their way to the Pacific shore are powerfully presented by Ken Burns in his 1997 documentary, *Lewis & Clark: The Journey of the Corps of Discovery.* The filmmaker's love of America and his award-winning cinematic skills combine to offer the viewer a riveting look at the thunderous rivers, majestic mountains, and undulating grasslands that so enraptured, and often threatened, the pathfinders. As historically grounded as it is visually appealing, the video can be purchased by contacting the dedicated people at PBS; their Web site is a good place to begin.

A growing number of Americans are attempting to identify and protect as many sites as possible for inclusion in the National Park Service's Lewis and Clark National Historic Trail that follows the transcontinental trek made by the Corps of Discovery. Working with the NPS, which also provides an extensive and inviting Web site about the Trail, are hundreds of private individuals who hope to add more locations to the list of documented places associated with the expedition's 8,000-mile journey. If you would like to get involved in this challenging and rewarding effort, contact the Lewis and Clark Trail Heritage Foundation, Inc., P.O. Box 3434, Great Falls, Montana 59404. Preserving more of the Corps' historic route would be a particularly fitting and memorable way to celebrate the 200th anniversary of an endeavor that changed how we look at ourselves as a nation.

5. Whose Civil War tactics are often studied by modern-day operatives as a "how to" manual of quick and effective guerrilla strikes?

A. Col. John Singleton Mosby, the "Gray Ghost of the Confederacy." One notable intelligence chief who found the lessons offered by Mosby especially useful was William Donovan. While working to establish the Office of Strategic Services, he sent an adjutant out to comb bookstores for any titles concerning the fabled Virginian. OSS Special Operations groups, in particular, were the beneficiary of Donovan's active interest in Mosby and his exploits: fighting behind the lines during World War II, these experts in sabotage and subterfuge employed many of the same tactics made famous (and infamous) throughout the Civil War by the Southern cavalry officer and his elite troop of partisan fighters. A number of respected books have been written about Mosby (even more are available now than at the time Donovan was collecting them). Your local library can provide you with some or most of these. Mosby's 1917 memoir was republished in 1987, and it is fascinating.

   For a more intimate insight into this legendary American, try visiting "Mosby's Confederacy" near Washington, D.C. Despite mounting development pressures, a good portion of the region still looks as it did when the Rebel rangers ruled the byways, frustrating Union regiments with countless lightning-fast and devastating raids. The John Singleton Mosby Heritage Area Association is working to preserve as much as possible of the Northern Virginia landscape where the colonel and his men operated. Established in 1995, the organization sponsors a variety of tours focusing on the Area's natural features and historic sites. The group has also produced several informative and educational publications that are free or cost very little. To become a member, write the John Singleton Mosby Heritage Area Association, P.O. Box 1178, Middleburg, Virginia 20118. The telephone number is (540) 687-6681.

Scout Bringing Information to Colonel Mosby, oil on canvas by Jean-Adolphe Beaucé, ca. 1868. In this painting, Mosby (center, with cape) listens as one of his scouts provides recently obtained intelligence regarding the location of a Union wagon train traveling from Harpers Ferry up the Shenandoah Valley to Winchester, Virginia. So successful were Mosby's stealth assaults against Federal supply lines and those guarding them that an infuriated Gen. Ulysses S. Grant ordered the Virginian captured and hanged without trial. Following the war, the two old soldiers formed a bond based on mutual respect and admiration. In his memoirs, Mosby recalled the grief he experienced upon learning of Grant's death in 1885. "I felt that I had lost my best friend," he wrote of his former adversary. *Courtesy The Museum of the Confederacy, Richmond, Virginia, with special thanks to Terri Hudgins. Photograph by Katherine Wetzel.*

6. Who is considered the first recorded African American woman to serve in the military and why?

A. Former slave Harriet Tubman. Using knowledge she gained while helping supervise the Underground Railroad in the South, the Maryland native served as a valuable scout and spy for the Union Army during the Civil War.

Known as the "Moses of Her People" for leading so many enslaved men, women, and children to freedom, Harriet was one of the Underground Railroad's most famous and successful conductors. Perhaps the best account of her remarkable life is a book she helped write following the Civil War, *Harriet, the Moses of Her People,* which was released in 1886. Many more publications focus on this intelligent, stalwart, and pioneering woman. Look for these titles at your local library. Also take advantage of the increasing amount of newly uncovered information about Harriet that is finding its way onto the next great "rail-road"—the Internet.

As for the Underground Railroad, it was arguably one of this country's most elaborate and productive covert ops (spook-speak for secret operations). If you are interested in pursuing the powerful story of this well-organized effort, you can learn along with others. Get involved in the growing movement to identify and document sites comprising America's highway to freedom.

One of the more inspiring initiatives was undertaken by Anthony Cohen, the great-grandson of a slave. In 1996, he retraced a 1,500-mile route to Canada used by many of those escaping bondage. His journal was posted on the Web site maintained by the National Parks and Conservation Association. With the National Park Service, the NPCA is one of the organizations working to establish a trail system formally incorporating many of the routes and buildings that were used by Harriet and others like her to shepherd an estimated 30,000 to 100,000 slaves to freedom.

Because of the clandestine nature of the Railroad and its mission, it is often difficult to prove that a particular house, barn, church, turnpike, or train track actually belonged to the extensive network made legendary by these courageous and defiant Americans. If you would like to help—or know of a structure in your neighborhood or state that may have been a stop on the Underground Railroad—log onto Anthony Cohen's North Star Web site. (The North Star was the heavenly body many traveling the Underground Railroad used as a natural navigational guide to lead them northward to a new life.) Be part of American history by helping to discover and protect an important chapter of it.

Another way to learn more about our country's lifeline to liberty is to visit the National Underground Railroad Museum in Maysville, Kentucky, a town noted for the numerous buildings located in and around it that have been identified as stations used by escaping slaves. The museum is both moving and educational. If you can't make the trip just yet, see something of the attraction's collection on the Internet.

Abolitionist and espionage agent Harriet Tubman. Several years following her service to the United States during the Civil War, the government awarded Harriet a monthly pension of $20. In his written testimonial to the former operative, Frederick Douglass took note of her work with the Underground Railroad: "The midnight sky and silent stars have been the witnesses of your devotion to freedom and of your heroism." *Courtesy Library of Congress (LC-USZ 62-7816), with special thanks to Mary Ison.*

7. While airplanes played a vital role in aerial combat starting with World War I, they were not actually introduced to wage what became known as "dog fights." What was the real reason planes were initially flown by both sides during the First World War?

A. For aerial reconnaissance to map the trenches constructed and used by the opposing sides during the conflict.

Because these intricate fortifications played such a crucial role in the overall conduct of the war, each army needed to know where the other's trench lines were located and if they had been expanded or reconfigured in any way (remember change detection from the "Signals and Signs" chapter?). Consequently, the first planes dispatched for military use during wartime were utilized as overhead observation and photographic platforms to monitor and map the trenches below. Aerial combat—dog fights—evolved when pilots flying defensive escort missions for reconnoitering aircraft engaged enemy planes performing the same duty for their air corps. (Germany's Red Baron was one of the most famous combat pilots of the era.)

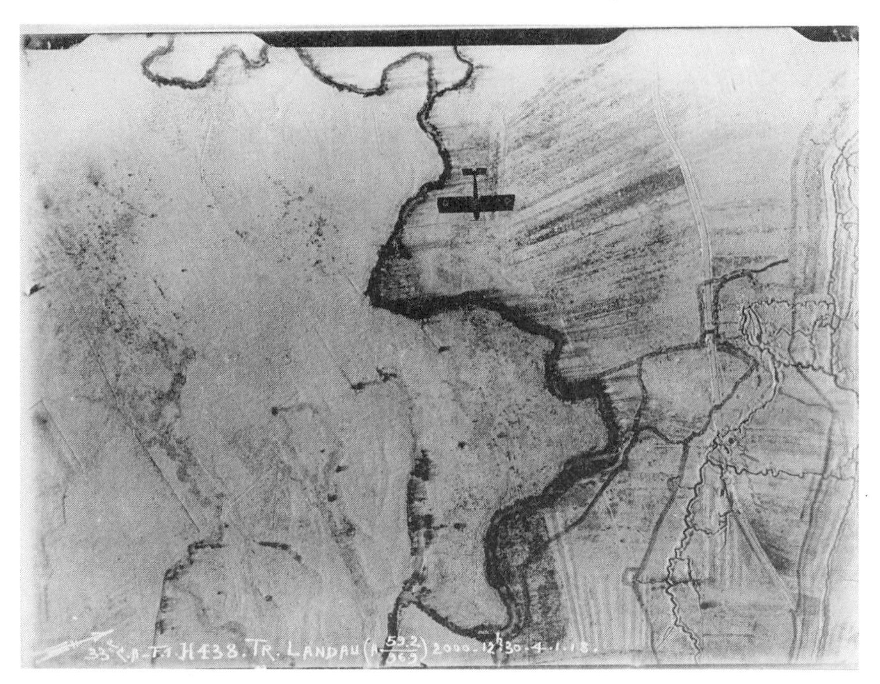

Aerial reconnaissance image taken by an Allied air crew on January 4, 1918. To the right, an intricate system of World War I trenches can be seen. Against the snow-covered terrain, cordite from recent shellings appears as black blotches. Shown near the top of the picture is the escort plane dispatched to protect the camera-equipped aircraft that was taking the overhead photographs. *Author's collection.*

8. What former OSS employee went on to a career after World War II that has terms such as braising, bulgur, flambé, and fleurons as part of its vocabulary?

A. Julia Child, star of the PBS television series *The French Chef* and author of several best-selling books about cooking and fine dining. During the Second World War, Mrs. Child was posted overseas with the OSS in Ceylon (now Sri Lanka) and China. She recently wrote, "I [had] a fascinating time and treasure my experiences with the OSS. We had some wonderful people." OSS veteran Betty McIntosh's book, *Sisterhood of Spies*, contains many amusing and enlightening stories about Mrs. Child's wartime service. Among her contributions, the Smith College graduate helped develop a shark repellent for OSS amphibious missions that was later used to protect space hardware after it landed in the ocean following reentry into the Earth's atmosphere.

9. What renowned director best noted for his Westerns helped the Allies advance their aerial photo reconnaissance efforts during World War II?

A. John Ford, who received two Academy Awards for best documentary while serving as head of the OSS's Field Photographic unit. In addition to directing the Oscar winners *December 7th* and *The Battle of Midway,* the famed cinematographer oversaw the expansion and refinement of U.S. aerial photo reconnaissance.

Using a Mitchell 35-mm motion-picture camera, Ford's men, several of whom were veteran Hollywood filmmakers he brought with him to the OSS, shot reel after reel of important military and industrial targets throughout the war. Prior to D-Day, these crews recorded miles of the French shoreline and the Atlantic Wall, which Hitler had constructed to protect the coast from a sea attack. This overhead imagery was used by Allied leaders while formulating plans for the invasion of Normandy on June 6, 1944. As Operation Overlord unfolded, Ford and his cameramen landed with the fighting units, chronicling the combined horror and bravery that marked the unparalleled event.

Fifty years later, another acclaimed director would draw inspiration from Ford's World War II documentaries while producing a motion picture now considered the most graphic and accurate depiction of D-Day ever presented. Steven Spielberg's *Saving Private Ryan* has as part of its historic and artistic legacy the pioneering work of John Ford and his OSS Field Photo group. Spielberg's DreamWorks company is helping restore some of Ford's wartime footage, which will be archived at the University of New Orleans' Eisenhower Center.

Hollywood's celebrated director goes to war. John Ford is shown here in 1940 training with some of the men he brought with him to the OSS. Before joining Donovan's intelligence organization, Ford and his crew had no official means of outfitting themselves for service. Not a problem. The filmmaker simply liberated the uniforms he needed from the Western Costume Company. Weapons for drilling were requisitioned from the 20th Century-Fox property department. *Courtesy the estate of John Ford.*

Name That HUMINT

Overhead photograph showing the invasion of Normandy on D-Day, June 6, 1944. Charged by Donovan with the responsibility for documenting the largest amphibious landing in the history of warfare, Ford regarded the assignment as the greatest honor of his life. *Author's collection.*

Ford's grandson Dan wrote an engaging and authoritative account of his grandfather's considerable achievements—including four more "civilian" Oscars for best director—that is as fascinating as the man himself. Titled *Pappy: The Life of John Ford,* the 1979 book offers a personal insight into the complex, gifted, and driven personality who put his lucrative Hollywood career on hold to serve in the OSS. Try to locate the book. It is well worth your time.

10. What star of *Dr. Strangelove,* considered by film critics and historians to be one of the best motion pictures of all time, served with the OSS and was awarded the Silver Star for his contributions to the war effort?

A. Sterling Hayden, who played Gen. Jack D. Ripper in the 1964 classic. An accomplished sailor, Hayden joined the Marine Corps after World War II began, actually breaking his contract with Paramount Studios to volunteer for duty. The actor's celebrity caused all kinds of problems for him and the military, so the New Jersey native legally changed his name to John Hamilton. (At the end of hostilities, he became Sterling Hayden the movie actor again.)

John Hamilton (aka Sterling Hayden) stands second from the right in the back row with some of his wartime colleagues. The citation accompanying the actor's Silver Star reads in part, "Captain Hamilton displayed great courage in making hazardous sea voyages in enemy infested waters, and reconnaissances through enemy held areas." *Courtesy CIA Exhibit Center.*

While with the OSS, Captain Hamilton commanded a fleet of schooners that ran the German blockade surrounding Yugoslavia, allowing much-needed arms and supplies to reach partisans fighting the occupying Nazis. Besides the sea, Hayden's other passion was writing. Despite the fact he did not graduate from high school, the man once described as the "prototype of the Jack London romantic" wrote two books. *Wanderer,* published in 1963, was autobiographical and took its title from the name of Hayden's beloved ship. The second, *Voyage: A Novel of 1896*, was widely received and chosen as a Book-of-the-Month Club selection for 1977. Both are worthy of a serious look by those wishing to understand more about this multifaceted matinee idol who also happened to be a certified war hero.

Studio still of Sterling Hayden. During a career that spanned some four decades, Hayden appeared in nearly 70 feature films, including *The Asphalt Jungle* and *The Godfather. Courtesy Catherine Devine Hayden, Wilton, Connecticut. Mrs. Hayden is the actor's widow.*

11. He was a successful jazz trumpeter who played with such notable bands as the Glenn Miller Orchestra. During World War II he served with the OSS in Europe and later joined the newly created Central Intelligence Agency where he became an expert on Middle Eastern affairs. Who was he?

A. Musician Miles Copeland. One of his sons, Stewart, was the drummer with The Police rock band for six years.

Miles Copeland's trumpet. Loaned by the musician's family for a special display sponsored by the CIA Exhibit Center honoring several OSS and early CIA veterans, the instrument accompanied Copeland overseas during his World War II intelligence service. Despite a lifetime of accomplishments in both the public and the private sectors, Copeland once confided, "I enjoyed playing big-band jazz more than I've ever enjoyed any vocation or avocation, before or since." *Courtesy CIA Exhibit Center.*

12. What OSS "member" was code-named "Cuthbert?"

A. Virginia Hall named her wooden leg Cuthbert. Following an escape on foot that took her across a mountain chain in the middle of winter, Virginia sent a message to her superiors in London saying, "Cuthbert is giving me trouble, but I can cope." Unaware of the problem-maker's true "identity," an official responded, "If Cuthbert is giving you trouble, have him eliminated." During her wartime career, Virginia was in constant need of an assortment of medical socks to cushion her leg against the prosthesis.

13. What historical landmark in Washington, D.C., served as headquarters for the OSS Topographical Model Section?

A. Ford's Theatre, where President Abraham Lincoln was assassinated. One of the World War II-era relief maps created by the OSS at Ford's is displayed in the CIA Library. It depicts the Italian peninsula and the neighboring island of Sicily.

14. Who is considered "Father of the CIA" despite the fact he never worked for the Agency?

A. Maj. Gen. William J. Donovan, who founded and headed the Office of Strategic Services during World War II. Historically and organizationally, the CIA is linked to the OSS and the trailblazing visionary who served as its only director.

A number of books are available that focus on the life and career of William J. Donovan. Like their topic, these works tend to be rather complex and imposing, but certainly worthy of the time and attention needed for a thoughtful look at the dynamic personality who oversaw the birth of our first formally chartered intelligence service. Check your library, especially its links to the Library of Congress, for selected titles.

One source that is particularly appealing is the 1919 first-person account written by Father Francis Duffy, the chaplain assigned to Donovan's World War I command, the legendary "Fighting Sixty-Ninth" Infantry Regiment of the New York National Guard. In *Father Duffy's Story,* the priest details much of the heroics that came to characterize the unit and its larger-than-life leader. The most decorated American officer to serve in the First World War, Donovan received the Medal of Honor for bravery under fire in France. The mind-numbing horrors he witnessed and endured during this time underscored to Donovan the need for a permanent and professional intelligence organization.

Father Duffy's book, while understandably somewhat biased, still offers the reader an insight into the world and events that led Donovan to press President Roosevelt for the creation of what would become the OSS during the next great global conflict barely two decades later. Continuing the lineage and legacy fostered by the man President Dwight Eisenhower called "the last hero," the Central Intelligence Agency was established in 1947 as the Cold War evolved and escalated.

Maj. Gen. William J. Donovan. This portrait hangs with those of every former Director of Central Intelligence along a dedicated wall in a corridor of the CIA Headquarters building in Langley. In addition, a towering statue of the general stands in the main lobby as part of the memorial established to recognize OSS members and their contributions to the nation during World War II. *Courtesy Central Intelligence Agency.*

15. What four future Directors of Central Intelligence (DCIs) served with the OSS during World War II?

A. The four OSS veterans were:

- Allen Dulles. For his contributions as head of the OSS station in Bern, Switzerland, Dulles was labeled "the greatest United States professional intelligence officer of his time" by the chief of General Eisenhower's intelligence staff. Dulles was the fifth DCI.
- Richard Helms. A onetime foreign correspondent who interviewed Adolf Hitler for a wire service story before the attack on Pearl Harbor, Helms later supervised OSS clandestine operations against the Nazis and their leader throughout Europe. Helms was the eighth DCI.
- William Colby. Among his other missions, Colby parachuted into occupied France with an OSS Jedburgh (special forces) team to help facilitate the D-Day invasion. Colby was the 10th DCI.
- William Casey. As chief of the OSS Secret Intelligence branch in London, Casey sent field agents behind enemy lines to collect information on German social, political, and economic matters, as well as on military and industrial targets. Casey was the 13th DCI.

16. What former DCI at various times served as a Congressman, Ambassador, Vice President, and then President of the United States?

A. George Bush, who is often called the "CIA's most distinguished alumnus." He was the 11th DCI.

17. What did the "U" in U-2 stand for? (Hint: this refers to the spy plane, not the rock band.)

A. Utility. The name was an attempt by engineers to mask the aircraft's real function, which was to obtain secret overhead photo reconnaissance of the then Soviet Union and many of its allies during the height of the Cold War. Imagery from U-2 flights showed President John Kennedy and his advisers that the Russians were providing Fidel Castro with an offensive nuclear capability only 90 miles from Florida, precipitating the Cuban Missile Crisis of October 1962.

18. What was the "Skunk Works" and what was its relationship to the U.S. aerial photo reconnaissance program?

A. "Skunk Works" was the designation given to that part of the Lockheed Aircraft factory in Burbank, California, where the U-2 and other high-performance planes were created and built.

The name was derived from a popular comic strip of the time, *Li'l Abner.* In it, Appalachian residents fashioned themselves brew masters, preparing potent concoctions into which they tossed just about anything, including old shoes and skunks. This created a stench that could be smelled for miles from the "Skonk Works," as the locals called the putrid place.

Similarly, the foul odor emanating from a plastics plant next to the super-secret area of the Lockheed facility where the planes were invented and manufactured reminded some of the comic strip's storyline. Reinforcing this perception were the special "concoctions" chief designer Kelly Johnson and his team of aeronautical engineers were cooking up for America's overhead reconnaissance effort.

19. What aircraft holds the official world records for air speed and sustained altitude?

A. The SR-71, called the Blackbird, with an air speed of Mach 3+ (more than 2,000 miles per hour) and a sustained altitude of 85,069 feet (over 16 miles). During a one-hour flight, a Blackbird can survey more than 100,000 square miles of the Earth's surface. Developed at the same "Skunk Works" that produced the U-2, different models of the SR-71 were designed as a newer generation of photo reconnaissance aircraft.

An actual Blackbird will be on permanent public display at the Smithsonian Institution's National Air and Space Museum Dulles Center at Washington Dulles International Airport in Northern Virginia when the facility is completed in a few years. (Another featured craft will be the *Enterprise,* America's first space shuttle.) Check the Air and Space Museum's Web site for the latest on this coming visitor attraction.

20. What is the ER-2?

A. The designation given to U-2s adapted for environmental missions. The ER stands for Earth Resources. Flown by NASA, these planes have been used in a variety of locales to help monitor and manage threats to a particular region and those inhabiting it. In Colorado, ER-2 overflights have helped track toxic heavy metal contamination flowing from silver, gold, zinc, and lead deposits mined and then abandoned over a century ago. Moreover, the introduction of infrared imagery taken during ER-2 missions has enabled firefighters to better determine the direction and intensity of raging wild fires that have plagued states like California and Florida.

America's premier photo reconnaissance aircraft: the U-2 (top) and the SR-71 Blackbird. Scale models of both planes are displayed at CIA Headquarters. They were presented to the Agency by Lockheed, home to the legendary and venerated Skunk Works. *Courtesy CIA Exhibit Center.*

21. Who is Jack Ryan and what actual area inside the CIA Headquarters building is now identified with him?

A. The principal intelligence officer in Tom Clancy's many espionage novels. Actor Harrison Ford, who has played Ryan in some screen adaptations of Clancy's books, was filmed using the badge machines in the main entrance of the CIA Headquarters building for the 1992 movie *Patriot Games.* Rent the video and look for the scene.

To learn more about some of the tradecraft used by agents throughout history, read H. Keith Melton's richly illustrated *The Ultimate Spy Book.* Melton, a private citizen who has assembled one of the most impressive and inclusive collections of espionage artifacts in the country, shares some of the more intriguing objects from his extensive holdings in this colorful hardback. Published in 1996, the book was widely received by adults and young people alike.

Many of the references cited in *Spies, Pop Flies, and French Fries* can be purchased over the telephone from Cloak and Dagger Books, probably the largest dealer of nonfiction intelligence-related titles in the country. New Hampshire resident Dan Halpin maintains an expansive inventory of publications covering the broad subject of espionage, with out-of-print works a specialty. And what he doesn't have, Dan the Book Man will try very hard to locate for you. Check his Web site for title availability and ordering information. Or give him a call at (603) 668-1629.

Finally, to "view" some of the items on display in the CIA Exhibit Center (which, because it is located in the Agency's secured headquarters building, is not open to the public), visit the CIA home page on the World Wide Web. Several pieces of intelligence-related artifacts are featured, along with a brief description of each, in a virtual tour of the Center we developed to bring some of its unique collection to the public. In addition, the Agency's home page serves as a good connector to similar sites, such as the one maintained by the National Reconnaissance Office, the government bureau that now oversees America's space-based surveillance programs.

IN CLOSING

A Word About Collections and Collecting

AFTER learning about some of the artifacts featured in the CIA Exhibit Center while I was curator, some readers might be interested in starting their own collection of "spy toys." To be sure, a number of original espionage-related gadgets can be purchased on the open market, principally through specialty catalogues and Internet auctions. This is particularly true of items that once belonged to intelligence services operated by the former Soviet Union and its allies. These relics can be fun and interesting to collect. Be careful, though, of older items offered for sale, especially those advertised as actual Civil War artifacts. Because of their popularity, authentic collectibles from this era can be very pricey and rare. In addition, there is the real problem of newly manufactured Civil War reproductions that are distressed (this simply means the finish is intentionally marred to look old) and then sold by unscrupulous individuals as original period pieces. The best advice is to know your dealer's reputation, and ask to see any documentation (such as bills of sale and written appraisals or family letters and photographs) that could verify an object's history.

One way many people have found to own a relatively inexpensive piece of Civil War-related memorabilia is to purchase several of the colorful limited-edition prints that have been released over the past decade or so. Collecting these can be a good way to learn more about this momentous time in our nation's history and decorate your walls at the same time.

A word of caution here, as well: some military artists do a better job than others of researching the scene they wish to paint, and, consequently, their works are more historically accurate. One of the most authoritative and respected artists currently painting Civil War battle scenes and personalities is Don Troiani of Historical Art Prints, Southbury, Connecticut. His signed and numbered prints can be found in better art galleries across the country. Popular periodicals dealing with military subject matter routinely carry advertisements for a variety of limited-edition prints that depict not only selected Civil War events and participants but also those from World War II and the Korean and Vietnam conflicts. Like other collectibles, military art can be enjoyed and then passed down to succeeding generations.

Index

Page numbers in **bold** indicate illustrations.

About the Author

LINDA McCarthy is a 24-year veteran of the Central Intelligence Agency who is credited with the creation of the CIA Exhibit Center, a museum of espionage-related artifacts situated in the Agency's Headquarters building in Langley, Virginia. As the Center's first curator, Linda spent nine years expanding its holdings from a handful of items to a widely respected collection of national and international intelligence memorabilia that has been featured in many print and broadcast media accounts.

During this time, Linda also designed and produced a number of special thematic displays for which she earned numerous commendations from Agency managers and praise from the directors of a variety of government and private-sector organizations. These covered such diverse topics as Civil War and World War I espionage operations, the bicentennial of the Constitution and Bill of Rights, the evolution of overhead reconnaissance, the contributions of African Americans to U.S. intelligence history, the 50th anniversary of D-Day, and the centennial of film director John Ford's birth.

In addition, Linda was recognized for her efforts in popularizing a number of lesser known individuals who made history while serving as intelligence operatives, two of whom, Virginia Hall and Morris "Moe" Berg, she writes about in this book.

To depict the life of Virginia Hall, Linda arranged for the first public display of the Distinguished Service Cross awarded to the World War II heroine, along with the field radio she used while working behind the lines in occupied France. Because of Linda's considerable knowledge about Virginia, authors and television producers often consult with her concerning the life and career of the woman who became one of the CIA's first female operatives when the Agency was established in 1947.

Another intelligence veteran Linda helped bring to the attention of the American public is the baseball player turned spy, Moe Berg. After 15 years in the major leagues, the enigmatic Moe served as an Allied agent during World War II, focusing on scientific targets. Working with a wide range of resources, including his declassified government file, Linda pieced together different parts of the Moe Berg story. Her extensive research led producers from NBC News, among others, to contact her for information about the former utility catcher who earned the Medal of Freedom for his wartime intelligence service. Following its broadcast in 1992, the piece, which featured an on-camera interview with Linda, earned the segment's producer an Emmy for "outstanding research." In recognition of her assistance to the highly acclaimed story, the producer then awarded the Emmy to Linda, making her the first (and so far only) CIA employee to receive such an honor.

While serving as Exhibit Center curator, Linda tried to make the collection as accessible to the public as possible. (Because the museum is located within the secured Agency compound, it is not open for tours.) Her 1993 interview on National Public Radio concerning Moe Berg was one of the most popular segments ever aired by NPR. Besides her many television appearances, including those on the *Today* show and *CNN's Real News for Kids,* Linda teamed up with several Agency employees to create a virtual tour of the Center that can be viewed by logging onto the CIA's home page.

Following her retirement in 1997, Linda embarked on a new career that invokes many of the stories and names associated with her tenure as the founding curator of the CIA Exhibit Center. As a professional speaker working through her own company, History is a Hoot, Inc., she brings the good news about inspirational Americans like Virginia Hall and Moe Berg to audiences all across the country. *Spies, Pop Flies, and French Fries* is her first book.

Linda, a 1973 graduate of George Mason University, Fairfax, Virginia, resides in the Shenandoah Valley. Much of her spare time is devoted to conservation causes, both historic and environmental. In 1991, she was named winner of the Civil War Society's Third Annual Anne D. Snyder Award for Battlefield Preservation.

To Order Additional Copies

Spies, Pop Flies, and French Fries:

Stories I Told My Favorite Visitors to the CIA Exhibit Center

By Mail: Please fill in the information below and send with your remittance (payable in U.S. funds only).

Name ______________________________

Address ______________________________

City ______________ State ________ Zip ________

MasterCard/Visa # ______________ Exp. ________

Check or money order enclosed for $ ________
(payable to History is a Hoot, Inc.)

Daytime telephone ______________

Quantity	**Unit Price**	**Subtotal**
______	$ 19.95	$ ________
	Deduct 10% when ordering 3 or more books	$ ________
	4.5% sales tax (VA only)	$ ________
	Shipping and handling*	$ ________
	Total Order	$ ________

*Shipping and handling depend on subtotal.

Subtotal	**Shipping/Handling**
$0.00–$19.99	$3.00
$20.00–$39.99	$4.00
$40.00–$59.99	$6.00
$60.00–$79.99	$8.00
$80.00–$99.99	$10.50
$100.00–$199.99	$13.50
$200.00+	Call for quote

This chart represents the total retail price of books only before applicable discounts are taken.

To Order By Telephone Using MasterCard or Visa, Please Call Toll Free 1 (877) 751-7129

Send order to:

History is a Hoot, Inc. • P.O. Box 285 • Markham, VA 22643-0285